INFORMATION TECHNOLOGY IN LIBRARY AND INFORMATION SERVICES

INFORMATION TECHNOLOGY IN LIBRARY AND INFORMATION SERVICES

Editor
Anuj Kumar Singh (A.K. Singh)
Assistant Professor-Library
Government Degree College
Jakkhini, Varanasi (U.P.)

Ess Ess Publications
New Delhi

INFORMATION TECHNOLOGY IN LIBRARY AND INFORMATION SERVICES

ISBN : 978-93-87698-12-3

First Published 2018

Published by:
Ess Ess Publications
4831/24, Ansari Road,
Darya Ganj,
New Delhi-110 002.
INDIA
Phones: 23260807, 41563444
Fax: 41563334
E-mail: info@essessreference.com
www.essessreference.com

Cover Design by *Patch Creative Unit*

Printed and bound in India

Dedicated to

My Beloved Parents

Babuji Late J.R. SINGH

Maa SMT. CHANDRAWATI SINGH

Contents

Preface

We are witnessing the phenomenon of exponential growth of scientific information, popularly known as "information explosion". The conventional tools available in the libraries and information centers are found inadequate in providing access to the existing information. As a result the gap between what is available and what is being communicated is increasing. This seriously affects the quality of research and decision-making. This situation cannot be allowed to continue. Techniques and processes of information management shall have to be re-oriented to enable a seeker to access his information conveniently and comprehensively. In this process of managing and communication of information, the present day technological advances are playing a vital role. Information Technology in fact has brought about a revolution in it.

Computer has changed the scenario of library work and services. It is now being used for the processing, consolidating and repackaging of information in a big way. Through telecommunication, information is transmitted from one point to another by use of electronic media. Telecommunication networks are there to handle digital machine readable data and to use telephone lines, micro waves and communication satellite to transmit such data. Now library networks provide communication lines for online conferences and seminars through digital data.

The world has become a global village with information superhighways created through networks like Internet. This has facilitated electronic librarian-ship with the diversification of library facilities and services to its user. The concept of virtual libraries OPAC, Hypertext, and teleconferences for the purpose of library and information services have become common.

The LIS services are changing fast in the face of new challenges and in response to new demands of the users and society. The advent of new technologies and their application to LIS work and services is accelerating and boost-up the new pace of this change. The era is popularly known as web-based knowledge and communication. Books and Journals have now been totally available online. NKN (National Knowledge Network) and NDL (National Digital Library), National Mission for Manuscript (NAMAMI) has now been changed the scenario of LIS services. Free availability of online e-journals and e-books has changed the mind setup of LIS communication and services. IT has paved the new way of servicing of LIS. That's why the new concept of library has emerged i.e. "Virtual Library"; "Digital Library"; "e-Library"; "Automated Library" or simply you can say "a library without walls".

The professionals and the users of libraries today are thus experiencing the transition from old LIS services to new LIS services i.e. information networks; from printed text to digital text; from limited boundaries to global access. Professionals must have required taking cognizance of this transition and redefining their role according to present situation. They must learn to adapt the changes. They must learn to manage chaos on the Web. They must have to come out from the traditional way of LIS services. They must have to change the way of CAS and SDI services. Nascent and prompt LIS services must have to provide to their users. They must have to be up-to-date from the latest tools and technologies of LIS services. They should not provide static and partial solution to dynamic and holistic problems. Professionals must follow the system's thinking and channelize their energies in the right direction for the sustainability and success of library for the future use.

The review team; Peer team or experts of Library Professionals must have meeting in an academic year and must discuss in depth about the betterment of LIS services by the use of latest tools and technologies i.e. Information Technology; available for up gradation of LIS services. No matter, most of the libraries have moved toward Digital Library but we are presently in infant position. We shall have to do more in this regards. Moving toward digital concepts, we should not forget to save the dignity of our profession. Concept of e-library has decreases the manpower in library profession. Librarianship and library professionalism must have its impact and originality. If librarianship is there, there will the emergence of library.

All the chapters contributed on various subthemes are informative and contains factual state-of-art of the subject in hand. I gratefully acknowledge my valuable contributors for their intellectual inputs and timely submission of the manuscript, and for the support and trust rendered by them. Nevertheless, the views, facts and figures reported and conclusions reached in their respective works are solely those of the contributors, and the editor does not owe any responsibility for them.

At the outset, I wish to express my reverence to the Supreme dignity God and my mother whose gracious blessings gave me the power of devotion and strength to compile this volume. I also express a deep sense of gratitude to my teachers, colleagues, students and my family especially my wife Mrs. Savita Singh extending knowledge based ideas and support where ever needed. I also extend my love to my sweet kids Ansh Pratap Singh and Aashee Singh for the patient throughout my journey of compilation the book.

I heartily propose my personal thanks to all the contributors for their enthusiastic and willing participation in this project. It gives me immense pleasure in presenting this work to the readers. I further hopeful, that the book grab the interest not only of the Library & Information Science professionals but also fulfill the demand of others professionals. If this book helps even a little bit in thought provoking and stemming ripples in the Library and Information Science professionals, the efforts of the contributors and editor will be suitable rewarded.

Varanasi (U.P.)

Anuj Kumar Singh
— *Editor*

ABOUT THE AUTHOR

Mr. Anuj Kumar Singh, B.A. (Hons), BLIS, MLIS, PGDCA, UGC-NET (Lib. & Info. Sc.) works as Assistant Professor in Library at Government Degree College, Jakkhini, Varanasi, Uttar Pradesh, India. He obtained all his degrees from Banaras Hindu University (BHU), Varanasi. Mr. Singh is actively associated with the Library and Information Science services, teaching, learning and research activities for more than 10 years. He has published 10 research papers and contributed chapters in journals and books of National and International repute. Mr. Singh has chaired many academic sessions and presented 32 papers in National and International Conferences and Seminars. He has also participated in 07 National and International reputed workshops and invited for delivering lectures series in different programs. He has good command over a lot of library software like CDS/ISIS, WINISIS, New GenLib+, SOUL, KOHA, DSpace, SLIM, GSDL, Libsys. Mr. Singh is the Life member of ILA, IASLIC, UPLA and UPPLA. He is also member in Board of Studies in many universities. He is also serving as Coordinator of several college level committees like RUSA, UPRTOU- study centre etc. He has supervised the Library Automation Project of Central Library, BHU under the firm Brilliant Barcode Solution, Kanpur, Uttar Pradesh. He has served as Guest Lecturer in the Dept. of Library and Information Science at MGKVP, Varanasi and Adhoc-Lecturer in the Dept. of Library and Information Science at MPGC, Mariahun, Jaunpur, Uttar Pradesh.

ABOUT THE BOOK

Today, we are living in the era of Information Explosive and in the world of Information Technologies. Each and every corner of our life has now been covered and affected by the use of IT. No one is untouched and incomplete today by the effectiveness of IT. The field of library and information science has now been great affected by the use of information technologies devices. Presently, each section of library has been using these technologies whether it is circulation section or technical section; book purchasing or periodical section etc.

The book **"Information Technology in Library and Information Services"** is totally related to the Library and Information Science Professionals. It is compendium of research papers offering a discourse towards the role that the how information and technologies has changed our library and information science services and has great influence on library users or society. The compilation of 18 empirical and conceptual papers, contributed by talented scholars and young library and information science professionals/scientists on the use of IT in library and information science services, examine how the IT operates, what is the effect, how it works on users, how users take its challenges, how much it is useful for our library, what is it cost-effectiveness, how can it regularize the services of library, how the services of library could be enhanced and the present statistical data. Expanded discussion presented by the author not only focus on emerging issues of modern Indian Libraries but also highlights deteriorating library and information science ethics and suggest ways to redeem a users conscious Library and Information services.

1

Bibliometric Analysis of Open Access LIS Journal "Trends in Information Management"

NG Thermi Moyon
Ph. D. Scholar, Deptt. of Library & Information Science, Mizoram University, Aizawl

Dr. Akhandanand Shukla
Assistant Professor, Deptt. of Library & Information Science, Mizoram University, Aizawl

ABSTRACT

Paper deals with bibliometric analysis of open access LIS journal Trends in Information Management for five years. During the period of study, journal had considerably poor number of research papers which were examined and analyzed in terms of distribution of articles, authorship pattern, degree of collaboration, geographical distribution of articles, forms of citations, and obsolescence of literature in the field. Study concludes with prevalent joint authorship pattern with higher degree of collaboration, India as the top most contributor of the articles for the journal and Jammu & Kashmir as the highest contributor amongst the Indian States, Journal Articles as the most prevalent source of information for writing research papers as well as used as citations, and more than 11 years of half-life for the journal citations.

Keywords : Bibliometrics, Open Access, DOAJ, Authorship Pattern, TRIM, Literature Obsolescence, Degree of Collaboration.

1. INTRODUCTION

Trends in Information Management (TRIM) is a bi-annual journal of the Department of Library and Information Science, University of Kashmir (Srinagar), J&K, India. It aims to publish original papers on various facets of information and knowledge management. The journal welcomes original articles, reviews of books, professional news etc. relevant to the focus of the journal (ICI World of Journals, n.d.). TRIM is open access journal and registered in DOAJ. Open Access (OA) brings revolution in online publishing and dissemination of scholarly research to its recipient. There are more than ten thousand journals from all disciplines that follow the mandate of Open Access. Open access publishing reduced the burden of copyright, licensing restrictions, and access fee at a large scale. Budapest Open Access Initiative (BOAI) was the first initiative to use the term "Open Access".

The open access journals are mostly supported by the academic institutions and research & development institutions or government grants for publishing these journals. Private publishers are publishing them with getting financial support from the authors and supporting from reputed companies or institutions or some of the funding agencies are providing support for the publishing open access journals (Tamizhchelvan & Dhanavandan, 2014). Bibliometrics study analyzes the research paper in terms of authorship, collaboration, geographical distribution, citation growth, obsolescence of literature, and other contributions by country or author. In 1917, Cole and Eale's study on the "history of comparative anatomy part-1: a statistical analysis" is considered to be the first bibliometric study. "The word 'Bibliometrics' first appeared in 1969 in Alan Pritchard's article 'Statistical Bibliography or Bibliometrics' in the December issue of the Journal of Documentation" (Hertzel, 2003). He described it as the "application of mathematics and statistical methods to books and other media of communication". In a later article, "bibliometrics and information transfer". Pritchard explained bibliometrics as the "metrology of the information transfer process and its purpose is analysis and control of the process".

2. REVIEW OF LITERATURE

There is a number of research conducted by various scholars in the field. Some of the relevant research conducted on the different aspects of bibliometrics have been reviewed and mentioned below:

Shukla & Moyon (2017) studied IRJLIS journal for five years and found that joint authorship is prevalent in the journal articles with 0.66 Degree of Collaboration, native country India is the top most contributor and Tamil Nadu is the highest contributor amongst Indian states. In a study, Shukla & Malsawmkimi (2017) found that "Library Philosophy and Practice" is the most productive LIS journal amongst open access LIS journals. Further, United States has been found as the most prolific country for LIS research. Shukla & Moyon (2016) studied "Annals of Library and Information Studies" and found that journal prevalent two authorship patterns with 0.61 degree of collaboration, India as the top most contributor of the research articles for the journal, New Delhi is the highest contributor amongst the Indian States, "Journal Articles" were found the most prevalent source of information for writing research papers and used as a citation, and calculated half-life of the journal citations found to be more than 10 years.

Gogoi & Barooah (2016) revealed in their study that papers from journals of Indian origin have greatly been used by the scholars and year-wise distribution of journals indicated that journal articles published during 2000-09 were highly preferred.

In the field of Chemistry, they found that researcher mostly cites works of 10-20 years old from recent and collaborative works were more than individual works. Awasthi & Jaiswal (2015) found the considerable increase in the archiving of library science journals over the years in DOAJ and print journals archive was more than online journals archive. Mondal & Saha (2015) conducted a study on the journal "JILA" and found the steady growth of publications during the study period and considerably positive degree of collaboration among authors. Further, it was found that majority of the authors belongs to one place only.

Verma et al. (2015) found no significant difference between solo research and collaborative research which tends to 0.51 degree of collaboration while journal was enriched with the scholarly contributions of 37 countries across the world. There are number of bibliometric studies conducted on "Annals of Library and Information Studies" by Hussain (2013), Lokhande (2013), and Pandita (2013) for different time periods and found that majority of the articles preferred two authorship pattern and major contributions were coming from India and specially from New Delhi. Similarly another LIS journal has been studied by Das (2013), and Roy & Basak (2013) for "Library Trends" and "Journal of Documentation" respectively; and found lower degree of collaboration for "Library Trends" while considerably prevalent joint authorship for "Journal of Documentation".

3. SCOPE OF STUDY

The scope is confined to the bibliometric analysis of open access Indian LIS journal "Trends in Information Management (TRIM)" for 5 years from 2011 to 2015.

4. OBJECTIVES OF THE STUDY

The objectives of the study are to:

(a) Examine the year-wise distribution of articles.

(b) Find the authorship pattern of the journal.

(c) Assess the degree of collaboration among authors.

(d) Find out geographical distribution of articles.

(e) Analyze the forms of documents cited in the journal articles.

(f) Determine the obsolescence of literature in the field.

5. HYPOTHESES

The hypotheses of the study are:

Hypothesis 1

H_0: There is no significant difference between solo research and collaborative research.

H_1: Solo research is less preferred than collaborative research.

Hypothesis 2

H_0: There is no significant relationship between time and growth of citation.

H_1: Time has an inverse relationship with the growth of citation.

6. RESEARCH METHODOLOGY

By using survey and observation methods of research, data has been collected from journal's website. A total of 35 research articles have been published during 5 years of study period. The bibliographical details of research articles were downloaded, tabulated, organized, and analyzed using MS-Excel and SPSS.

7. DATA ANALYSIS

(a) Year wise Distribution of Articles

Table 1: Distribution of Articles – Year wise

Year	Vol. No.	No. of Issues	No. of Contributions	%
2011	7	2	21	60
2012	8	2	10	28.57
2013	9	-	-	
2014	10	1	4	11.42

2015	11	-	-	
Total		**5**	**35**	**100**

(***Source:*** Primary Data)

Table 1 displays the total number of articles published in 5 issues of 5 volumes from the year 2011-2015 published in the journal TRIM. The journal "TRIM" is not regular in terms of publication, so that observed very less number of research papers during study. On the observation of Table 1, it has been found that major contributions of research papers to the journal in Volume 7 (60%) and Volume 8 (28.57%). Volume 10 has the lowest publication percentage (11.43%) of total articles observed in the journal during study period. There are two volumes that have not a single publication and further it has been observed that other volumes also do not have sufficient number of published articles.

(b) Issue wise Distribution of Articles

Table 2. Distribution of Articles - Issue wise

Issues (Month)	**Volume Number 7**	**8**	**9**	**10**	**11**	**Total**	**%**
June	5	5	-	-	-	10	28.57
December	16	5	-	4	-	25	71.42
Total	**21**	**10**	**-**	**4**	**-**	**35**	**100**

(***Source:*** Primary Data)

Table 2 indicates issue wise publications of articles in five volumes. On the observation, it has been found that during June issue there was less number of publications to the journal (28.57%) than December issue (71.42%).

(c) Authorship Pattern

Table 3. Authorship Pattern of the Journal

Year	Volume	No. of Authors				Total	Total
		One	Two	Three	Four	Articles	Author (%)
2011	7	2	13	5	1	21	47(66.19)
2012	8	5	3	2	-	10	17(23.94)
2013	9	-	-	-	-	-	-
2014	10	1	3	-	-	4	7(9.85)
2015	11	-	-	-	-	-	-
Total		**8**	**19**	**7**	**1**	**35**	**71(100)**
Percentage22.85		**54.28**	**20**	**2.85**	**100**		

(*Source:* Primary Data)

Table 3 shows authorship pattern of research contributions published in the journal during 2011-2015. On the observation of Table 3, it has been found that 22.85% articles published in the name of one (single) author of the total publications in journal. There were 54.28% articles published in the name of two authors of the total publications while 20% articles published in the name of three authors of total publications to the journal. There were only 2.85% articles published in the name of four authors. From the analysis, it has been inference that two authorship pattern is most prevalent in the journal followed by single authorship and three authorship respectively. Further, Table 3 also reveals the total number of authors i.e. 71 contributed 35 research papers to the journal. Out of total number of authors, 66.19% belongs to Volume 7 of the journal followed by Volume 8 (23.94%), Volume 10 (9.85%).

(d) Degree of Collaboration

The Degree of Collaboration (C) of the contributors has been derived using the Subramanyam formula:

$$\text{Degree of Collaboration (C)} = \frac{Nm}{Nm + Ns}$$

Where, C = Degree of Collaboration

Nm = Number of multiple authors

Ns = Number of single authors

C = = or C = 0.77

The Degree of Collaboration has been calculated for the year 2011-2015. Single author contribution is 8 and multiple authors' contribution is 27. Volume wise Degree of Collaboration of the journal falls in the range of 0.5 to 0.90. The Degree of Collaboration of the journal is 0.77 which very good sign for having more collaborative research among authors of the journal.

Table 4. Degree of Collaboration among Authors

Year	Volume	Single Author(Ns)	Multi Authors (Nm)	Total Ns + Nm	Degree of Collaboration
2011	7	2	19	21	0.90
2012	8	5	5	10	0.5
2013	9	-	-	-	-
2014	10	1	3	4	0.75
2015	11	-	-	-	-
Total		**8**	**27**	**35**	**0.77**

(***Source:*** Primary Data)

(e) Geographical Distribution of Articles

Table 5. Geographical Distribution of Articles

Year	National	International	National+ International	Total No. of Articles
2011	19	2	-	21
2012	9	1	-	10
2013	-	-	-	-
2014	4	-	-	4
2015	-	-	-	-
Total	32	3	-	35
Percentage	**91.42**	**8.57**	-	**100**

(***Source:*** Primary Data)

Table 5 displays geographical distribution of articles in the journal. The articles have been divided into three categories: **National, International, and National + International.** On the observation, it has been found that 91.42% articles were belongs to national contribution and 8.57% were belongs to international contribution. National contribution is more than international contribution to the journal. There were no contributions to national and international collaboration. On the analysis, it has been found that since the journal is of Indian origin, highest number of articles submitted and published by India in the journal. International contribution of articles to the journal is less than national because of geographic distance as well as less popularity, weak presence, irregularity in publication of the journal.

(f) Country-wise Distribution of Authors

Table 6 shows country wise distribution of authors. India has the highest number of contributors (90.14%) to the journal followed by Nigeria (4.22%), U.K., Saudi Arabia, Malaysia and Canada (1.4% each). The journal has 9.86% authors from other countries and rests were from India which displays its weak international acceptance and presence amongst LIS professionals. Among foreign countries authors, 42.8% authors belong to Nigeria only that indicates Nigerian authors have more interest in publishing their research papers with Indian journal TRIM.

Table 6. Country wise Distribution of Authors

Rank	Country	No. of Authors	Percentage
1	India	64	90.14
2	Nigeria	3	4.22
3	U.K.	1	1.40
4	Saudi Arabia	1	1.40
5	Malaysia	1	1.40
6	Canada	1	1.40
Total		**71**	**100**

(***Source:*** Primary Data)

(g) State-wise Distribution of Indian Authors

Table 7. State wise Distribution of Indian Authors

Rank	Name of State	No. of Authors	Percentage
1	Jammu & Kashmir	33	51.56
2	Uttar Pradesh	5	7.81
3	Karnataka	4	6.25
4	Gujarat	4	6.25
5	Punjab	4	6.25
6	Maharashtra	4	6.25
7	Tamil Nadu	3	4.68
8	Uttarakhand	2	3.12
9	Rajasthan	2	3.12
10	New Delhi	1	1.56
11	Assam	1	1.56
12	Meghalaya	1	1.56
Total		**64**	**100**

(***Source:*** Primary Data)

Table 7 shows state wise distribution of Indian authors. Jammu and Kashmir (51.56%) has the highest number of contributors to the journal followed by Uttar Pradesh (7.81%), Karnataka, Gujarat, Punjab and Maharashtra (6.25% each), Tamil Nadu (4.68%), Uttarakhand and Rajasthan (3.12% each) etc. Indian contributors to the journal belong to 12 states and union territories of India which shows journals less circulation, availability and acceptance amongst Indian LIS professionals.

(h) Forms of Documents Cited

The study has been conducted to know the prevalent forms of citations appeared in research articles published in the journal. From the analysis of Table 8, it has been found that "Journal Articles" were most prevalent in terms of citations/references in research articles. There were total 565 citations received to 35 research articles published in the journal during study period, and more than 46.01% citations belong to Journal Articles, followed by Books and Reference Sources (16.46%), Web based Resources (13.62%), articles published in Conference/ Seminar Proceedings (13.27%), Research/ Project Reports (3.18%), and Theses/ Dissertations (0.88%). By the analysis of the Table 8, it has been inference that "Journal Articles" are the first choice as a citation/reference for writing a research paper by authors. Books and Reference Sources have been second choice of authors for citation due to having conceptual and historical information & knowledge about the topic of research. Web based Resources are recent in origin and have been third choice of authors for citation in the articles. Conference/ Seminar Proceedings have been used as the source of information and knowledge for research purposes but less than Web based Resources due to availability problem in comparison to Web based Resources. Though Conference/ Seminar Proceedings are older than Web based Resources but authors, nowadays, wants information sources in their fingertips which are not fulfilled by Conference/ Seminar Proceedings. Research/ Project Reports and Theses/ Dissertations have been used less by researchers to write the research papers in the field, and it might be due to less/ restricted availability of such infoımation sources in public domain.

Table 8. Forms of Documents Cited in the Articles

SN	Forms of Document	Total No. of Citations	Percentage
1	Journal Articles	260	46.01
2	Books and Reference Sources	93	16.46
3	Web based Resources	77	13.62
4	Conference/ Seminar Proceedings	75	13.27
5	Miscellaneous Items	37	10.13
6	Research/Project Reports	18	3.18
7	Theses/ Dissertations	5	0.88
Total		**565**	**100**

(***Source:*** Primary Data)

(i) Chronological Distribution of Citations

Table 9. Chronological Distribution of Citations

Years	Journal Articles	Books and Reference Sources	Web based Resources	Conference/ Seminar Proceedings	Misc. items	Research Project Reports	Theses/ Dissertations	Total
Upto-1980	5(1.92%)	7(7.52%)	-	-	1(2.70%)	1(5.55%)	-	14(2.47%)
1981-1990	11(4.23%)	3(3.22%)	1(1.29%)	1(1.33%)	-	1(5.55%)	1(20%)	18(3.18%)
1991-2000	49(18.84%)	24(25.80%)	4(5.19%)	13(17.33%)	3(8.10%)	4(22.22%)	-	97(17.16%)
2001-2010	172(66.15%)	58(62.36%)	40(51.94%)	60(80%)	30(81.08%)	11(61.11%)	4(80%)	375(66.37%)
2011-2015	23(8.84%)	1(1.07%)	32(41.55%)	1(1.33%)	3(8.10%)	1(5.55%)	-	61(10.79%)
Total	**260**	**93**	**77**	**75**	**37**	**18**	**5**	**565**

(***Source:*** Primary Data)

The chronological distribution of citations to the journal articles has been given in Table 9. The citations from the journal articles have been divided into 5 time frames having periodicity of 10 years each. The citations before 1980 were enclosed within the cluster upto 1980 and citations after 2010 to 2015 enclosed in 2011-2015 groups. From the Table 9, it has been observed that TRIM research papers prefer most of the citations of 2001-2010 (66.37%), 1991-2000 (17.16%), and 2011-2015 (10.79%) time periods. It indicates that 94.32% literature cited in the research papers of the TRIM are within the period of 1991-2015 i.e. last 25 years duration. Further categorically, citations belongs to Journal Articles covered from 2001-2010 (66.15%), 1991-2000 (18.84%), and 2011-2015 (8.84%). Within the Journal Articles category, 93.84% citations are within the period of 1991-2015. Citations in the form of Books and Reference Sources also have 62.36% citations within 2001-2010, 25.8% within 1991-2000, and 3.22% within 1981-1990 time periods. The majority of citations (91.39%) are within 1981-2010 time periods in case of Books and Reference Sources. The Web based Resources as form of citations appeared during 1981-1990 time period first time in the journal articles and all the citations are within 1981-2015 time periods. The major contribution of citations (93.5%) in the form of Web based Resources are within 2001-2015 time periods i.e. last 15 years. In case of Conference/ Seminar Proceedings, 80% citations are within 2001-2010 followed by 17.33% from within 1991-2000 time periods. In this case, 97.33% citations are within 1991-2010 time periods. In the case of Miscellaneous Items (97.29%), Research/ Project Reports (88.88%) and Theses/ Dissertations (80%), major citations are within 1991-2015 time periods. From the analysis, it has been inference that literatures older than 25 years (published before 1991) have not been used more by researchers and they have tendency to use latest literature published in any form. Further Journal Articles for writing research papers (for citing purposes) are prevalent amongst authors/ researchers followed by Books and Reference Sources, Web based Resources, and Conference/ Seminar Proceedings.

(j) Obsolescence of LIS Literature

Table 10. Frequency of Citations and their Obsolescence

Years	Journal Articles	Books and Reference Sources	Web based Resources	Conference/ Seminar Proceedings	Misc. items	Research/ Project Reports	Theses/ Dissertations	Total Citations (f)	Cumulative Citations (Cf)
1-10	98(37.69%)	23(24.73%)	57(74.02%)	29(38.66%)	17(45.94%)	6(33.33%)	1(20%)	231	231
11-20	137(52.69%)	51(54.83%)	19(24.67%)	43(57.33%)	19(51.35%)	9(50%)	3(60%)	281	512
21-30	14(5.38%)	10(10.75%)	1(1.29%)	3(4%)	-	2(11.11%)	1(20%)	31	543
31-40	8(3.07%)	5(5.37%)	-	-	-	-	-	13	556
41-50	3(1.15%)	1(1.07%)	-	-	1(2.70%)	1(5.55%)	-	4	560
51-60	-	2(2.15%)	-	-	-	-	-	3	563
61-70	-	1(1.07)	-	-	-	-	-	2	565
Total	**260**	**93**	**77**	**75**	**37**	**18**	**5**	**565**	

(*Source:* Primary Data)

Table 10 displays frequency of citations appeared in the articles published in the journal IRJLIS and obsolescence of literature cited in those articles. The total 565 citations were classified into 7 time zones, each having the time duration of 10 years. These 565 citations were also categorized according to their form of document. From the Table 10, categorically different rates of obsolescence observed for different forms of documents. For example, for Journal Articles, Books and Reference Sources, Conference/ Seminar Proceedings, Miscellaneous Items, Research/ Project Reports, and Theses/ Dissertations rate of obsolescence is up to 20 years whereas in case of Web based Resources rate of obsolescence is only up to 10 years. The calculated rate of obsolescence or half-life of citations to the journal is 11.21 years.

(k) Testing of Hypotheses

Hypothesis 1

H_0: There is no significant difference between solo research and collaborative research.

H_1: Solo research is less preferred than collaborative research.

Solo Research	Collaborative Research
8	27

Chi Square (ξ^2) is a test to test the significance when obtained data are expressed in frequencies or percentage or proportions.

	Observed Frequency (fo)	Expected Frequency (fe)
Solo Research	8	17.5
Collaborative Research	27	17.5

Computation of ξ^2 with the data given in above Table 11.

Table 11. Computation of ξ^2 for TRIM

	fo	*fe*	*fo - fe*	*(fo – fe)²*	*(fo – fe)²/ fe*
Solo Research	8	17.5	-9.5	90.25	90.25/17.5=5.15
Collaborative Research	27	17.5	9.5	90.25	90.25/17.5=5.15
Total	**35**	**35**		**180.5**	**180.5/17.5=10.31**

Degree of Freedom (df) = (R-1) (C-1) = (2-1) (2-1) = 1.

From critical value of Chi-Square table, the values of X^2 distribution for 1 degree of freedom at .05 and .01 level are 3.84 and 6.64 respectively. The calculated X^2 value is 10.31 which is greater than critical X^2 value 3.84 at .05 level. This value is significant and so null hypothesis is rejected and it proves that solo research is less preferred than collaborative research.

Hypothesis 2

H_0: There is no significant relationship between time and growth of citation.

H_1: Time has inverse relationship with growth of citation.

Table 12. Correlation of TRIM

Correlations			
		Time (Year)	**Citations**
Time (Year)	Pearson Correlation	1	-.550**
	Sig. (2-tailed)		.000
	N	129	129
Citations	Pearson Correlation	-.550**	1
	Sig. (2-tailed)	.000	
	N	129	129

**. Correlation is significant at the 0.01 level (2-tailed).

There is a significant adverse (negative) relationship between time and growth of citations (r= -.550, significant at .01 level). Therefore, null hypothesis (H_0) is rejected and accepted alternative hypothesis (H_1). Thus, it proved that time has inverse relationship with growth of citation. The correlation have been measured between time and citations and found that there is significant adverse (negative) relationship for TRIM journal. This proves the alternative hypothesis that time has inverse relationship with growth of citations to the journals. As time passes in backward movement (from 2015-1950-1900), there should be more number of citations from recent to old but it is not so, and if time passes in forward movement (1900-1950-2015), there should be more number of citations from old to recent. But in both the conditions, it has been found adverse correlation between time and growth of citations.

8. RESEARCH FINDINGS

The analysis of the data collected through survey and observation have revealed a number of findings on open access LIS journal "TRIM" from India which are as follows:

1. The journal has published 35 articles in 5 issues of 5 volumes from the year 2011-2015. The journal was not regular in terms of publication, so that observed very less number of research papers during the study. With the available data, Volume 7 has published major percentage of research papers to the journal i.e. 60% whereas Volume 10 has the lowest publication percentage i.e. 11.42%.
2. As per issue wise publications of articles in five volumes, it has been found that journal publishes only two issues in a year and December issue (71.43%) of the journal has the highest number of published articles than June issue (28.57%).
3. In the study of authorship pattern of the journal, it has been found that two authorship pattern (54.28%) is most prevalent in the journal followed by single authorship (22.85%). Further, study also reveals that 71 authors contributed 35 research papers to the journal, out of which 66.19% authors belongs to Volume 7 of the journal followed by Volume 8 with 23.94% authors.
4. The Degree of Collaboration for the journal has been

calculated for the year 2011-2015. The Degree of Collaboration for the journal is 0.77 which indicates significant amount of collaborative research among authors of the journal.

5. In the analysis of geographical distribution of articles in the journal, it has been found that majority (91.42%) of research papers were belong to national contribution whereas 8.57% research papers belongs to international contribution. There were no research papers that have national and international collaboration. Since the journal is of Indian origin, so highest number of research papers submitted and published by Indian authors in the journal. International contribution of research papers to the journal is very less than national and it might be due to geographic distance, less popularity of the journal as well as irregular publication cycle.

6. Further, analysis based on country wise distribution of authors, it has been observed that India has the highest number of contributors (90.14%) to the journal. The journal has 9.86% contributors from overseas which display its very less international reach, distribution, acceptance and presence amongst LIS professionals. Nigerian authors (42.8%) have more interest in publishing their research papers in the journal amongst all overseas authors. In the terms of number of foreign countries, the journal has covered only 5 overseas countries as its widespread availability for publication of the research papers.

7. Further, analysis based on state wise distribution of authors within India, it has been observed that Jammu and Kashmir (51.56%) has the highest number of contributors to the journal followed by Uttar Pradesh (7.81%), Karnataka, Gujarat, Punjab and Maharashtra (6.25% each), and Tamil Nadu (4.68%). Indian contributors to the journal belong to only 12 states and union territories of India which shows journals less circulation, availability and acceptance

amongst Indian LIS professionals.

8. The study has been conducted to know the prevalent forms of citations appeared in research articles published in the journal and found that Journal Articles (46.01%) were most prevalent in terms of citations/references in research articles followed by Books and Reference Sources (16.46%), Web based Resources (13.62%), Conference/ Seminar Proceedings (13.27%), and Miscellaneous items (10.13%). Research/ Project Reports and Theses/ Dissertations were less cited by researchers to write research papers in the field.
9. The study has been conducted to know the chronological distribution of citations to the journal articles and found that research papers published in the journal prefer most of the citations of 2001-2010 (66.37%), 1991-2000 (17.16%), and 2011-2015 (10.79%) time periods. It indicates that majority (94.32%) of literature cited in the research papers of the journal were within the time period of 1991-2015 i.e. last 25 years duration.
10. The study has been conducted to determine the rate of obsolescence (half-life) of LIS literature in the journal and found that the calculated rate of obsolescence (half-life) for the journal is 11.21 years.
11. From the testing of significance of Hypothesis 1 with Chi-Square test, it has been found that journal prefer collaborative research than solo research.
12. From the testing of correlation between time and growth of citations in Hypothesis 2 with Pearson Correlation, it has been found that journal has significant adverse relationship between time and growth of citations and thus alternative hypothesis is accepted.

9. CONCLUSION

The journal "TRIM" found to be irregular in terms of timely publication as well as issues also. Collaborative research is preferred in journal articles with higher Degree of Collaboration among authors. The native country and native state contribution is more than others which shows poor popularity within the country. Since, journal is most famous in the native country and state, so native authors/ researchers are the major contributors of research papers to the journal. Moreover, the journal's overseas publicity is very poor which denotes its poor international visibility and acceptance. Within the native country, journal covered 12 states and more than half of authors/ contributors were belong to native state. The "Journal Articles" become the most prevalent source of information for writing the research papers (Shukla & Moyon, 2016 & 2017). Journal articles records recent references which were not older than 25 years (published before 1991) from the today (Shukla & Moyon, 2016 & 2017). The rate of obsolescence of literature has been found more than 11 years in the journal. Further, collaborative research found more than solo research whereas time has an inverse relation with the growth of literature. From the other studies conducted by Shukla & Moyon (2016, 2017) and observations from the present study, it has been established that Indian open access LIS journals have similar trends in terms of national and foreign contribution of articles, forms of documents cited in the journal, use of recent information sources and increase in the trend of collaborative research.

REFERENCES

Awasthi, Shipra, & Jaiswal, Babita. (2015). Library and Information Science journals in DOAJ: a bibliometric study. *International Journal of Scientific & Engineering Research*, 6(8), 1476-1481.

Budapest Open Access Initiative. (2002). Retrieved on May 25, 2018, from http://www.budapestopenaccessinitiative.org/

Das, Tapas Kumar. (2013). A bibliometric analysis of contributions in the journal 'Library Trends'. *Library Philosophy and Practice*. Retrieved on September 1, 2016, from http://digitalcommons.unl.edu/libphilprac/1014/

Directory of Open Access Journal (DOAJ). Retrieved on May 26, 2018, from https://doaj.org/search?source

Gogoi, Manisha, & Barooah, Pronab Kumar. (2016). Bibliometric analysis of Indian Journal of Chemistry, Section B to study the usage pattern of information in the field of Material Science. *Library Philosophy and Practice*. Retrieved on September 1, 2016, from http://digitalcommons.unl.edu/cgi/viewcontent.cgi?article=3519&context=libphilprac

Hertzel, Dorothy H. (2003). Bibliometrics History. *In* Drake, Miriam A. (Ed.), *Encyclopedia of Library & Information Science* (2nd ed. Vol. 1, pp. 288-328). New York: Marcel Dekker.

Hussain, Akhtar (2013) Annals of Library and Information Studies: a bibliometric analysis.

Journal of Library Metamorphosis. Retrieved on September 28, 2016, from https://www.researchgate.net/publication/259195305

ICI World of Journals. (n.d.). ***Trends in Information Management.*** Retrieved May 27, 2018, from https://journals.indexcopernicus.com/search/details?id=33989

Lokhande, Rahul S. (2013). Content analysis of open access LIS journal "ALIS" (2002-2011). *E-Prints*. Retrieved on January 26, 2016, from http://eprints.rclis.org/18283/

Mondal, D. & Saha, S. (2015). Journal of Indian Library Association during 2008-2014: a bibliometric study. *Journal of Indian Library Association,* 51(1), 27-33.

Pandita, Ramesh. (2013). Annals of Library and Information Studies (ALIS) journal: a bibliometric study (2002-2012). *DESIDOC Journal of Library & Information Technology,* 33(6), 493-497.

Roy, S. B., & Basak, M. (2013). Journal of Documentation: a bibliometric study. *Library Philosophy and Practice*. Available at http://digitalcommons.unl.edu/libphilprac/945

Shukla, Akhandanand & Malsawmkimi (2017). Mapping of Open Access Library and Information Science Journals on Scopus: A Scientometric Assessment. *In* Singh, S. K. et al. (Eds), Proceedings of 1st International Conference on Transforming Library 2017, Kokrajhar (pp. 504-517). Guwahati: MRB Publishers.

Shukla, Akhandanand & Moyon, NG Thermi. (2017). International Research - Journal of Library and Information Science: A Bibliometric Analysis. *Library Philosophy and Practice (e-journal)*. 1530. Available at http://digitalcommons.unl.edu/libphilprac/1530

Shukla, Akhandanand & Moyon, NG Thermi. (2016). Bibliometric Assessment of Scholarly Communications of Annals of Library and Information Studies (ALIS). *Library Waves*. 2(2), 68-79.

Tamizhchelvan, M., & Dhanavandan, S. (2014). A study on open access journals from South Asian countries registered in DOAJ. *International Research: Journal of Library and Information Science*, 4(3), 443-456.

Verma, Anjali, Sonkar, S. K., & Gupta, Vibha. (2015) A bibliometric study of the Library Philosophy and Practice for the period 2005-2014. *Library Philosophy and Practice*. Paper 1292. Available at http://digitalcommons.unl.edu/libphilprac/1292

2

Status of ICT Infrastructure in College Libraries of Aizawl City : A Study

Dr. Akhandanand Shukla
Assistant Professor, Deptt. of Library & Information Science, Mizoram University, Aizawl – 796 004

S. Sialai
M. Phil. Scholar, Deptt. of Library & Information Science, Mizoram University, Aizawl – 796 004

ABSTRACT

Paper deals with the current ICT infrastructure available in ten college libraries of Aizawl city. A well prepared structured questionnaire was distributed to college librarians of select libraries. The study analyzed the status of ICT facilities available in college libraries of Aizawl city and suggested the best practices for increasing the ICT application in college libraries. The study reveals the lack of sufficient fund for libraries which affects the development of ICT infrastructure in college libraries. Lack of sufficient library staff and ICT skilled staff are another valid reasons for poor ICT infrastructure. State government should take initiative towards the development of ICT infrastructure in college libraries of Aizawl city.

Keywords : Information and Communication Technology, College Library, ICT Infrastructure.

1. INTRODUCTION

ICT stands for "Information and Communication Technologies," refers to technologies that provide access to information through telecommunications. It is similar to Information Technology (IT) but focuses primarily on communication technologies. This includes the Internet, wireless networks, cell phones, and other communication mediums (TechTerms, 2010). The phrase ICT has been used by academic researchers since the 1980s, but it became popular after it was used in a report to the UK government by Dennis Stevenson in 1997 and in the revised National Curriculum for England, Wales and Northern Ireland in 2000 (Wikipedia, n.d.). In the past few decades, ICT has provided society with a vast array of new communication capabilities. For example, people can communicate in real-time with others in different countries using technologies such as instant messaging, voice over IP (VoIP), and video-conferencing. Modern ICT has created a "global village", in which people can communicate with others across the world as if they were living next door (TechTerms, 2010).

"The implementation of new and advanced technologies in the libraries requires competent staffs with different ICT skills. One of the important factors for successful implementation of ICT is the level of competence of the staff working knowledge of ICT skills for library professionals for handling various library functions to make full use of this potential for handling various library functions. To make full use of this potential in library management, it is essential that libraries should have adequate professionals who have the thorough knowledge of ICT application in libraries but in practice, most of the library professionals do not have the adequate skill of ICTs" (Verma, 2014).

The application of ICT on library basically employs on its

routine functions like acquisition, technical processing, circulation, periodical management, stack verification, digitization and other maintenance works of the library. To save the time of the user as well as library workers, nowadays, computerization work is very much important for the library. ICT provides such platform through which librarians can provide enhanced and very much improved library services to their users well in time. In present day scenario, libraries, as well as librarians, have to face many challenges, some of them are:

- Change in the information needs of the users
- Change in the information habit of the users
- The openness of libraries to people (with OPAC, Websites, & Social Networks), and
- Networking which has made possible to expand access to resources.

To cope up with the above-mentioned challenges, the libraries have to employ ICT infrastructure. Another side, libraries have shown progress over the past few years due to the application of ICT based tools and technologies in their services & facilities.

2. LITERATURE REVIEW

Lata & Singh (2014) surveyed the status of ICT infrastructure in Health Information System which included previous exercises to map ICT in the health sector in developing countries, white papers, technical reports, research reports on the aspects of ICT and public health, policy issues-related, and evaluations in this area. Seena & Pillai Sudhier (2014) studied the ICT skills amcng library professionals in the Kerala University library system and revealed that majority (88.6%) of the library professionals are skilled in Windows operating system whereas management of electronic resources is reasonably known to 51.9% professionals. Among Web 2.0 technologies, email/ instant messaging on chat was frequently used by 85.9% professionals, and wishes were frequently used by 69.1% professionals. Praveen

Kumar (2013) studied the application of ICT in state libraries of Haryana and Chandigarh and concluded that library automation is one of the effective and efficient applications of ICT. Ruan & Qiang (2013) conducted a study to know the role of information technology in academic libraries' resource sharing in Western China and revealed the economic inequalities in the Eastern and Western Regions of China. The study shows that the information sharing resources are huge in Eastern China whereas in Western Regions it is less due to insufficient funds. Although in the eastern region, it is well-provided funds from the central government which is lacking in the Western Region of China. Due to this, the students face problems in Western China in terms of ICT infrastructure. There is a great demand to the central government to provide more fund and ICT infrastructure to the western region equally with the eastern parts for the development and growth of the country through CALIS. Vanden Elzen & Roush (2013) studied the gaming programs for the students in the academic libraries. It plays a very important role for the students for their higher education the libraries not only need to focus on instructing students about library resources but also need to actively reach out to them by integrating gaming programs in academic libraries. This study also reflects the integration of games in academic libraries in Wisconsin, USA and the staff of the university library has been successfully incorporating games into library outreach programming. It shows the effective results to the students efficiently by offering such kind of video gaming in the university libraries. It also studies the partnership for planning games as well as the marketing and impact results on its users.

Davendra & Nikam (2012) studied the use of OPAC and WebOPAC by the users at Law University in Karnataka and revealed that the rate of success of locating the document of their interest from OPAC was 75%. Significantly, the satisfaction level of the users was high with the OPAC facilities. Maan (2012) studied the usages of ICT products and services in Adesh Institute of Engineering & Technology, Faridkot, Punjab and revealed the use of ICT products and services by the students and staff of the institute. The study demonstrated and elaborated the usages of ICT products and services such as how they search from the library? Whether they are satisfied with the online services provided by the library? How the problems faced by the users? And suggestions have been given to make the library services more effective and efficient to cater the information needs of the students and other users. There is a significant difference in the use of e-resources by the university library users. Pandya et al. (2012) assessed the current content alerts through RSS feeds and found that the alert service using RSS feeds providing as a part of current awareness service targeting the current information needs of the users. Information push service is one of the most important functions of a library consisting of electronic resources. They have also highlighted on the do's and don'ts of RSS technology. Thanuskodi (2012) examined the use of the Internet by the faculty members of Arts and Science Colleges in Cuddalore described by the frequency of Internet use, the purpose of using the Internet, use of different Internet services and impact of the Internet on research/ teaching. A questionnaire was prepared and sent to 70 faculty members of the college. The result indicated that 58.62% of respondents access the Internet from college library and 91.37% respondents indicated that research and teaching is the primary purpose of using the Internet. Murugusan & Balasubramani (2011) conducted a study to inspect the application of ICT in the library for research and development in Tamil Nadu and provides recommendations to give priority to digital library initiatives; consortia based subscription to enhance the effective and efficient use of ICT in the library for research and development in Tamil Nadu. Kamba (2011) studied the implication of ICT in libraries of higher education institutes in Africa and exposed the ICT impact on libraries of higher education. The study analyzed the efforts made by the higher education's libraries in Africa to recognize, re-structure and re-oriented the library facilities and personnel with ICT adoption. In addition, the study also highlighted the various efforts to establish networking and consortia among the libraries and the implications that could be derived by applying ICT into higher education's libraries. The study concluded the reasons why ICT application is taking a snail speed in library development in Nigeria and provided solutions as a panacea for library development in Africa.

3. SCOPE OF STUDY

The scope of the study was limited to the college libraries of Aizawl city. There are 10 college libraries in Aizawl city which are given below with their abbreviated names:

1. Pachhunga University College Library (PUC)
2. Government Aizawl College Library (GAC)
3. Government Hrangbana College Library (HBC)
4. Government Aizawl West College Library (GAWC)
5. Government Aizawl North College Library (GANC)
6. Government T. Romana College Library (TRC)
7. Government Zirtiri Residential Science College Library (ZRSC)
8. Government J. Thankima College Library (JTC)
9. Government Johnson College Library (GJC)
10. Mizoram Law College Library (MLC)

4. OBJECTIVES OF STUDY

The objectives of the study are:

(a) To assess the status of ICT facilities available in college libraries of Aizawl city.

(b) To assess how many information professionals are trained in the handling of ICT.

(c) To identify the limitations of the libraries in using ICT based services.

(d) To suggest the best practices for increasing the ICT application in college libraries.

5. METHODOLOGY

The survey method has been found appropriate to conduct the study. For the data collection, a structured questionnaire was framed for the college librarians to ascertain the infrastructures developed by the library to provide the library services. A considerable amount of information on the resources, facilities, and services of college libraries were collected from their printed brochures and official websites etc.

6. DATA ANALYSIS & INTERPRETATION

A. Funding Source of Institution & Separate Library Budget

Table 1 shows that majority (90%) of colleges of Aizawl city funded by the State Government and only one college i.e. Pachhunga University College is funded by Central Government. The libraries also receive their fund through colleges which belong to State Government. There is lack of separate library fund/ budget for collection development and for the development of ICT infrastructure.

Table 1. Funding Source of Institution (N=10)

Funding Source	No. of Institutions (%)
State Govt.	9 (90%)
Central Govt.	1 (10%)

B. Availability of Library Website & Separate Library Building

Table 2 gives information about the colleges of Aizawl city whether they were having separate library website/ webpage or not. The result shows that 60% college libraries were having a library website whereas 40% libraries were not having the separate website. Further, Table 2 reveals the status of college library building of ten colleges of Aizawl city. The result shows that most of the college libraries (60%) in Aizawl city don't have a separate library building whereas 40% college libraries were separated from the college's main building and have the separate building.

Table 2. Presence of Library Website & Library Building (N=10)

Response	Library Website (%)	Library Building (%)
Yes	6 (60%)	4 (40%)
No	4 (40%)	6 (60%)

C. Sitting Capacity & Working Hours of Library

Table 3 gives information about the sitting capacity of the users in the college libraries of Aizawl city. From the analysis, it has been found that majority of libraries (80%) are having the sitting capacity of less than 50 readers at a time. There are few libraries (20%) having more than 50 readers sitting capacity. Only one college library has sitting capacity up to 200 which was the highest among all of the college libraries. All the college libraries of Aizawl city open for 8 working hours in a day. There is no library which exceeds more than 8 working hours in a day.

Table 3. Sitting Capacity of Library (N=10)

Sitting Capacity Range	No. of Libraries (%)
Up to 50	8 (80%)
51-100	1 (10%)
101-150	0
151-200	1 (10%)
201-250	0

D. Professional Qualifications of Librarians'

On the analysis of librarian's highest professional qualifications, it has been found that majority (60%) of librarians have qualified Masters Degree in Library Science whereas only 20% have Ph. D. in LIS and 10% have M. Phil. in LIS. There is only 10% librarians have Bachelor Degree in Library Science.

Table 4. Librarians' Professional Qualification

Highest Professional Degree	No. of Librarians (%)
Diploma in LIS	0
Bachelor in LIS	1 (10%)
Master in LIS	6 (60%)
M Phil in LIS	1 (10%)
Ph.D. in LIS	2 (20%)

E. Staff Availability in Library

Table 5. No. of Library Staff

Name of College	Professionals	Semi-Professionals	Professional with IT Competence	Non-Professional	Total Library Staff
GTRC	1	0	0	1	2
HBC	1	1	0	2	4
GAC	1	0	3	0	4
GJC	1	1	0	0	2
GAWC	1	1	0	1	3
PUC	1	2	6	2	11
ZRSC	1	1	0	1	3
GANC	2	0	0	1	3
MLC	1	1	0	1	3
GJTC	1	0	0	2	3
Total	**11 (28.94%)**	**7 (18.42%)**	**9 (23.68%)**	**11 (28.94%)**	**38**

Table 5 shows the staff strength of the ten college libraries of Aizawl city. It has been observed that PUC is having 6 professional staff with IT competence and the Government Aizawl College also having 3 professionals but the rest of the college libraries don't have IT professionals. There is an availability of professionals with every college library but some college libraries do not have non-professional staff also.

F. Status of E-Documents in Library

On the analysis of Table 6, it has been found that all the college libraries lack the sufficient electronic documents collection whether it is available in any form. Only one college library i.e. Govt. Hrangbana College Library had the sufficient number of e-journals from the country and from the foreign also. No college library has access facility to any databases. Audio/visual materials like CDs/DVDs are also not available up to satisfactory level.

Table 6. Status of Library Collection

College Library	Audio/Visual Cassettes/CDS	Indian E-Journals	Foreign E-Journals	Databases
GTRC	6	0	0	0
HBC	4	200	700	0
GAC	0	0	0	0
GJC	0	0	0	0
GAWC	0	0	0	0
PUC	0	0	1	0
ZRSC	0	0	0	0
GANC	20	0	0	0
MLC	15	0	0	0
GJTC	0	0	0	0

G. Information Searching Pattern in Library

Table 7 display the way of locating the reading materials of college libraries. Due to technological advancements, OPAC search has been found most prevalent in every library than direct search on shelves. No user is searching the literature through catalogue card and they have the last choice to consult with the library staff.

Table 7. Way of Searching Pattern

Search Method	No. of Library (%)
Through Catalogue card	0
Through OPAC	10 (100%)
Direct Search on Shelves	4 (40%)
With Help of Library Staff	2 (20%)

H. Computerization of Circulation System

From the analysis of Table 8, it has been observed that most of the college libraries (50%) were computerized so that they have computerized circulation process in the library. Only 10% college libraries have the manual system of circulation process whereas 40% libraries were following both systems i.e. manual method & computerized system of circulation.

Table 8. Computerization of Circulation System (N=10)

Status of Circulation System	No. of Library (%)
Computerised	5 (50%)
Manual	1 (10%)
Both	4 (40%)

I. Computerized Services offered by Library

Table 9 shows the ICT based services offered by college libraries. The CAS service was offered by 50% college libraries whereas only 10% libraries were offered SDI services to their users. Majority of college libraries (80%) were offering photocopy services to their users.

Table 9. Computerized Services of Library (N=10)

Services	No. of Library (%)
CAS	5 (50%)
SDI	1 (10%)
Photocopy	8 (80%)

J. Library Automation Status

Table 10 shows the current status of library automation of college libraries. On the analysis, it has been found that majority (90%) of college libraries was automated and only 10% were not automated. Further, in response to the query regarding software used by the college libraries, it has been found that all the 9 automated libraries (100%) have been used SOUL 2.0 software for library automation. In relation to the automation completion timing, it has been found that majority (78%) of college libraries automated after the year 2010 whereas 22% college libraries were automated before the year 2010. Similarly, level of automation was responded by the librarians and it has been found that out of 10 college libraries, the majority (90%) of college libraries were partially automated whereas 10% were under computerization process. There was no library with fully computerized status.

Table 10. Automation Status of Library (N=10)

Library Automated	No. of Library (%)
Yes	9 (90%)
No	1 (10%)

On the analysis of Table 11, it has been observed that all the nine automated libraries (100%) have computerized "circulation section", 56% automated "cataloguing section", and 44% have "OPAC" facility. There were few libraries (22%) that have automated "acquisition section" and only 11% have automated "serial control management".

In response to the barcode implementation, it has been found that only 10% of college libraries do not have barcode facility for library functions whereas the majority (90%) of college libraries has implemented the barcode in their libraries. Further, on use of barcode in the functioning of the library, it has been found that all the automated college libraries (N=9) were using barcode for circulation work whereas 22% libraries were utilizing it for annual stack verification work. Beyond these two works, there is no other utilization option of barcode found in the libraries.

Table 11. Sections Computerized in the Library (N=9)

Sections Computerized	No. of Library (%)
Acquisition	2 (22%)
Circulation	9 (100%)
Serial Control	1 (11%)
Cataloguing	5 (56%)
OPAC	4 (44%)

K. Internet Connectivity in Library - Status

Table 12 shows the availability of Internet connection in the college libraries of Aizawl city. There were 90% college libraries which have the Internet connection whereas 10% do not have the Internet connection in their libraries. Further on the use of the Internet (N=9), it has been observed that majority (78%) of the college libraries were using the Internet for official work as well as information search for the users. For the resource sharing, only 33% college libraries were using the Internet whereas 56% college libraries were using the Internet for online database searching for users.

Table 12. Internet Availability in Library (N=10)

Having Internet Connection	No. of Library (%)
Yes	9 (90%)
No	1 (10%)

L. Computer's Availability in Library – Status & Use

Table 13 shows the availability of computers in the college libraries. On the observation of computer's availability, it has been found that 20% college libraries have less than 5 computer machines in their library whereas 10% college libraries have 11-15 computers. The majority (60%) of libraries have 6-10 computers. There were 10% college libraries that have more than 20 computers in their library. Further in response to the number of Internet connections in the library, it has been found that majority (56%) of college libraries have Internet connections up to 5 machines whereas 44% college libraries have Internet connections on 6-10 machines.

Table 13. Computer's Availability in Library (N=10)

No. of Computers	No. of Library (%)
Less than 5	2 (20%)
Between 6 - 10	6 (60%)
Between 11 - 15	1 (10%)
Between 16 - 20	0
Between 21 - 25	1 (10%)

M. Campus LAN – Status & Use

Table 14 shows that 30% of the college libraries have Campus LAN facility whereas rest of the 70% college libraries does not have Campus LAN facility. Further, all the college libraries that have Campus LAN (N=3), they have the facility to provide e-resources availability over Campus LAN.

Table 14. Campus LAN Availability in Library (N=10)

Having Campus LAN	No. of Library (%)
Yes	3 (30%)
No	7 (70%)

N. Library Networks Membership – Status & Use

Table 15 displays the results of the membership status of the college libraries of Aizawl city. There were 80% college libraries have professional membership whereas 10% does not have any professional membership. Interestingly 10% libraries do not have responded to the question. Further on the type of professional organization's membership, it has been found that 62.5% of college libraries (N=8) have joined the INFLIBNET membership and equally also joined N-LIST. There were 25% libraries does not have any response to the question.

Table 15. Library Networks Membership (N=10)

Having Membership	No. of Library (%)
Yes	8 (80%)
No	1 (10%)
No Response	1 (10%)

O. Library Consortium – Usefulness

A consortium is very much important for the library through which it can share and enrich their electronic resources, but only 30% college libraries found it to be useful for them and rest of 70% college libraries had no response to the question. Further, to enquire how consortium is useful for libraries? No librarians have given any response to the query. On the query that whether resource sharing minimizes the cost of library materials? All of the college librarians have accepted that resource sharing minimizes the cost.

Table 16. Usefulness of Consortium (N=10)

Is Consortium Useful	No. of Library (%)
Yes	3 (30%)
No	0
No Response	7 (70%)

P. Library Services Improvement by using ICT

Table 17 shows the improvement of library service through the use of ICT and finds out that 70% of the college libraries have improved their services due to ICT implementation and only 20% of them did not much agree with the service improvement through ICT implications. 10% college libraries have no response to the question.

Table 17. Library Service Improvement due to ICT (N=10)

Are services improved due to ICT	No. of Library (%)
Yes	7 (70%)
No	2 (20%)
No Response	1 (10%)

Q. RFID Application in Library

Table 18 shows the application of RFID in the college libraries of Aizawl city and found that most of the college libraries (90%) were not having RFID and only 10% college libraries have implemented RFID application in libraries. Further, to know the future plan to adopt RFID application (N=9), only 22% responded to have RFID in future whereas 78% have no plan to adopt RFID in future.

Table 18. Status of RFID Application (N=10)

Having RFID	No. of Library (%)
Yes	1 (10%)
No	9 (90%)

R. Skilled Library Staff to Manage ICT Tools

Table 19 reveals the status of skilled library staffs availability in the college libraries of Aizawl city and found that majority (70%) of college libraries does not have skilled staff to manage ICT based resources & services. There are only 30% college libraries that have the skilled staff to manage ICT based resources & services.

Table 19. Skilled Library Staff Availability (N=10)

Having Skilled Staff	No. of Library (%)
Yes	3 (30%)
No	7 (70%)

S. Reasons for Lacking of Skilled Library Staff

On the analysis of reasons behind the lack of skilled library staff in college libraries of Aizawl city, it has been found that there is lack of proper ICT based training to library staff, lack of ICT competent staff, and lack of a number of staffs in the college libraries. Further, on planning for ICT training, it has been found that only 30% college libraries have future plan to train their library staff whereas 60% college libraries do not have any future plan whereas 10% college libraries have no response to the question. Moreover, in terms of planning of ICT training to staffs, college libraries (N=3) have two ways to provide ICT based training to their library staffs. All the college libraries (N=3) have the plan to organize ICT based training in their college whereas 33% college libraries have the plan to send the library staff outside for training also if the need arises.

In an answer to the question, it has been found that 60%

college librarians (N=10) were not satisfied with the present ICT infrastructure available in the library whereas only 30% librarians were satisfied with the availability of ICT infrastructure in college libraries. There are 10% college librarians which have not responded to the question. Further, to investigate the reason for dissatisfaction with the current ICT infrastructure in college libraries, librarians have responded that they are facing the problem with the number of ICT skilled staff in the library and lack of sufficient ICT infrastructure in the college libraries.

T. Future Plan for ICT based Services in Library

In response to the question, college librarians have given their views with regards to future plan for the development of ICT based services in their library. Some important future plans given by the librarians have been listed below:

i. To improve library resource sharing.

ii. To make library fully automated.

iii. To increase the use of networked-based resources including online databases, e-journals, and e-books.

iv. To make the library security RFID enabled, using of smartcard and launching of the separate library website.

v. To upgrade the automation software as per requirement.

vi. To provide Internet search facility on more no. of computers in the library.

vii. To have a separate library building for enhancing the library services and facilities.

U. Suggestion for Improving Libraries ICT Infrastructure

In response to the question, college librarians have suggested improving college libraries ICT infrastructure as given below:

i. Recruitment of ICT skilled professional staff.

ii. Recruitment of more number of skilled professional staff.

iii. A separate budget for developing ICT infrastructure in the library.

iv. Organization of ICT training program for library staff.

7. FINDINGS OF THE STUDY

The major findings of the study are:

(a) Except for one college library, other 9 college libraries are funded by the state government. Due to getting insufficient fund from state government, libraries have no proper ICT infrastructure in the college library.

(b) The majority (60%) of college libraries have separate library website.

(c) Most of the college libraries (60%) of Aizawl city don't have their own library building which creates the problem in the growth of the library. Further, the majority of college libraries (80%) are having less sitting capacity i.e. up to 50 readers at a time; and college libraries of Aizawl city open for 8 hours in a day which is an ideal situation but it may be increased for the users.

(d) On the analysis of librarian's highest professional qualifications, the majority (60%) of librarians have qualified Masters Degree in Library Science whereas only 20% have Ph. D. in LIS and 10% have M. Phil. in LIS.

(e) In terms of professional staff in the library, only one college library has 6 professional staff with IT competence and other college libraries are facing staff problem.

(f) None of the college library is getting separate library fund/ budget from the authority for the development of ICT infrastructure.

(g) All the college libraries are lacking with the sufficient electronic resources.

(h) Due to technological advancements, OPAC search has been found most prevalent in every college library than direct search on shelves. There are 50% college libraries that are having computerized service. CAS service is offered by 50% college libraries whereas 10% college libraries offering SDI services to their users. Majority of college libraries (80%) are offering photocopy services to their users.

(i) The majority (90%) of college libraries is partially automated and 100% college libraries are using SOUL 2.0 library automation software. Further, the majority (78%) of college libraries automated after the year 2010.

(j) There are 90% college libraries that have an Internet connection and out of that majority (78%) of the libraries are using it for official work as well as information search for the users. The Internet is used for resource sharing by 33% college libraries and 56% college libraries are using the Internet for online database searching. In terms of Internet connection, 56% college libraries have Internet connections up to 5 machines whereas 44% college libraries have Internet connections on 6-10 machines.

(k) The majority (60%) of college libraries have 6-10 computers in the library. There are only 10% college libraries which have more than 20 computers in their library.

(l) There are 80% college libraries which have professional membership whereas 10% does not have any professional membership. Out of them, 62.5% have joined the INFLIBNET & N-LIST membership. There are 30% college libraries which have found consortium as a useful resource.

(m) The majority (70%) of college librarians have accepted that they have improved their services due to ICT implementation. Further, majority (90%) of college libraries does not have RFID system and only 22% have planned to implement RFID in future.

(n) There are 70% college libraries that do not have ICT skilled staff to manage ICT based resources & services. Lack of proper ICT based training to library staff, lack of ICT competent staff, and lack of the number of staffs in the college libraries are the major problem for lack of ICT trained staff. Further, only 30% college libraries have future plan to train their library staff and the majority (67%) of college libraries have plan to organize ICT based training in their college itself whereas only 33% college libraries have plan to send them outside for ICT based training.

(o) The majority (60%) of college librarians are not satisfied with the present ICT infrastructure available in their library.

8. CONCLUSION

ICT plays a very vital role in the faster dissemination of library resources to their users. Lack of ICT infrastructure in college libraries affects negatively in the development of information resources and services. Lack of ICT skilled library staff is also one of the barriers in providing information services to users on right time. Insufficient funding for the library development breaks the continuous growth of the library. With proper government funding and special initiatives for ICT infrastructure development in college, libraries will certainly uplift the poor status of library development in all terms. Timely and ICT skilled library staff recruitment may also make the library condition healthier. In the present scenario, ICT infrastructure is one of the important factors to attract the library users and librarians should also take the positive initiative from their side to uplift the status of the library in all terms.

REFERENCES

Davendra & Nikam, K. (2012). OPAC and user perception in law university libraries in the Karnataka: a study. *International Journal of Information Dissemination and Technology. 2*(4), 301-306.

Kamba, Manir A. (2011). Application of ICT's in libraries of higher education institutes: a panacea catapulting library development in Africa. *Journal of Library & Information Technology, 31*(1), 65-71.

Lata Suresh, & Singh, Surya Nath. (2014). Status in ICT and health information system. *International Journal of Information, Library and Society, 3*(1), 16-24.

Maan, I. S. (2012). Usages of ICT products and services: a case study of Adesh Institute of Engineering & Technology, Faridkot (Punjab). *International Journal of Information Dissemination and Technology,* 2(4), 296-300.

Murugusan, N. & Balasubramani, R. (2011). Application of ICT based resources and services in research and development libraries in Tamil Nadu. *European Journal of Social Sciences, 23*(1), 157-164.

Pandya, J. D., Patel, S.S., & Poluru, L. (2012). Current content alerts through RSS Feeds: a web 2.0 approach. *International Journal of Information Dissemination and Technology, 2*(4), 278-286.

Praveen Kumar. (2013). Application of ICT in public libraries: a study of central state library of Haryana and Chandigarh. *SRELS Journal of Information Management, 50*(1), 93-100.

Ruan, L. & Qiang, Z. (2013). The role of information technology in academic libraries' resource sharing in Western China. *Library Trends. 62*(1), 180-204.

Seena, S. T., & Pillai Sudhier, K. G. (2014). A study of ICT skills among library professionals in the Kerala University Library System. *Annals of Library and Information Studies, 61*, 132-141.

TechTerms. (2010). *ICT*. Retrieved May 4, 2018, from https://techterms.com/definition/ict

Thanuskodi, S. (2012). Use of Internet by the faculty members of Arts and Science College in Cuddalore district, Tamilnadu, India: a case study. *International Journal of Information Research, 2*(2), 207-225.

Vanden Elzen, A. M. & Roush, J. (2013). Brawling in the library: gaming programs for impactful outreach and instruction at an academic library. *Library Trends, 61*(4), 802-813.

Verma, M. K. (2014). Information Communication Technology (ICT) Challenges for Library Professional: A Professional Approach. *In* Singh, M. P. et al. (Eds.), *Libraries: Towards Digital Paradigm* (pp.354-363). Faizabad: Bharati Publishers.

Wikipedia. (n.d.). *Information and communications technology*. Retrieved May 5, 2018, from https://en.wikipedia.org/wiki/Information_and_communications_technology

3

Citation Analysis of Journal Collection Building (2008-2017)

Vaishali. B. Kanekar
Research Scholar, Dept. of Library & Information Science
Dr. Babasaheb Ambedkar Marathwada University, Aurangabad. (MS)
Dr. Siddiqui Eraj Azeeza
Librarian, Dr. Rafiq Zakaria College for Women,
Aurangabad. (M.S.), India

ABSTRACT

The present study is based on the citation pattern of the Collection Building, E-Journal. Ten Volumes of the journal containing 40 issues from 2008 -2017 have been taken into consideration for the present study. The study is based on 3748 references appended to 211 articles contributed by the authors in Collection Building. In Authorship pattern it was found that Solo Researchers with 2259 (60.2%) are Predominant than Collaborative Researchers with 1490 (39.7%), the year wise distribution of references was high i.e. 562 (14.9%), Journals are in the first position with 2014 (53.7%), followed by Books, Conference. The Degree of collaboration (DC) of publication between the year of ranges between 0.26 (2008) and 0.51 (2017) with an average of 0.39. USA ranked first with 2741 (73.1%), followed by India, UK. "Collection Building" scores the 1st rank which account to 136 (6.75%) of the total Citations followed by Journal of Academic Librarianship. Year of distribution of citations which shows that 2552 (34.8%) the highest number of Citations out of a total of 3748. Maximum no. of Print citations 3073 (81.9%) whereas 675 (18 %) are electronic citations.

Keywords : Citation, Collection Building, Degree of collaboration.

INTRODUCTION

Citation analysis is one of the important tools among other information techniques to find out the important journals in a particular field and is becoming popular in their practical application in libraries and information centers. Citation analysis is mathematical analysis of references of citation appended at the end of each scientific communication as an essential part of it. Citation analysis as a tool is used to identify the core reference in a subject by counting the citations appended at the end of each scientific article. It is basically a technique, which involved the process of collection, counting, analysis and interpretation of citations given in research writing and thereby helping in identification of signification sources of information.

Collection Building was selected as the source journal for the present research study. The journal was started in 1973. The journal is published by Emerald Group Publishing. Its publication frequency is four issues per year. Collection Building aims to provide well-researched and authoritative information on collection development for librarians in academic, public, school and special libraries. It offers expert analyses of resource development, technology and resource sharing.

REVIEW OF LITERATURE

Nishat (2017) highlighted on Business Research. It covers 18 issues of 9 volumes of Business Research published bi-annually during the period 2008-2016. The study reveals that researchers have cited journals (77.33%) more than books, editorial works and all other sources of information. Growth in collaborative trend of writing papers is also noticed as citations contributed by two authors is (37.67%) and single authors is (33.42%) followed by three authors (21.59%).

Singh & Singh (2017) investigated the citation and authorship patterns of International Journal of Library and Information Studies on the basis of Google Scholar. Google scholar has covers the broad areas of the scholarly literature out of world. This study is a part of google scholar, which covers the field of LIS. This article gives the Study found that inside a five years term (between2011-2015) 20 articles are 118 times cited in the GS.

Verma et al. (2016) in their study analyzed the citation pattern of the articles published for the period 2005–2014 of the Library Philosophy and Practice, E-Journal. 1180 articles are published in the journal during 2005-2014. Highest numbers (198) of articles were published in 2011. The EJournal contained 20978 references for the study period of which 15518 are documentary sources citations and 5460 are non-documentary source citations.

OBJECTIVES OF THE STUDY

1. To identify the Year-wise distribution for citations per article.
2. To identify the authorship pattern of references per articles.
3. To identify the year-wise degree of collaboration.
4. To identify the form-wise distributions of references.
5. To find out the country-wise distribution of cited references.
6. To identify the core journals of most cited citations.
7. To find out the chronological distribution of citations.
8. To find out the Distribution of E-Citations and P-Citations

DATA ANALYSIS

Table 1. Year-wise distribution of citations per Articles

Year	Volume No.	No. Of Articles	No. of Citations	% of Citations
2008	27(1-4)	24	469	12.9
2009	28(1-4)	24	223	5.94
2010	29(1-4)	24	412	10.9
2011	30 (1-4)	24	232	6.18
2012	31(1-4)	22	276	7.36
2013	32(1-4)	20	375	10
2014	33(1-4)	18	459	12.2
2015	34(1-4)	18	335	8.93
2016	35(1-4)	18	405	10.8
2017	36(1-4)	19	562	14.9
Total	/	**211**	**3748**	**100**

From table find out the references per article during 2008 to 2017 was 3748. It observed that the highest number of references per articles in 2017 i.e. 562 (14.9%), followed 459 (12.2%) citations in the year of 2014. While the lowest number of references per article showed in the years of 2009 and 2011, respectively.

Table 2. Authorship Pattern

Authorship	2008	2009	2010	2011	2012	2013	2014	2015	2016	2017	Total	%
Single Author	343	131	265	136	156	240	332	193	192	271	2259	60.2
Two Author	68	48	74	38	47	78	57	67	124	131	732	19.5
Three Author	16	13	21	18	23	29	22	30	26	63	261	6.96
Four Author	5	7	10	8	5	3	7	9	8	26	88	2.34
More than Four Author	5	1	2	7	9	14	9	11	30	34	122	3.25
Unidentified	32	23	40	25	36	11	32	25	25	37	286	7.63
Total	**469**	**223**	**412**	**232**	**276**	**375**	**459**	**335**	**405**	**562**	**3748**	**100**

Table 2 indicates that the details about the authorship pattern 2259 (60.2 %) articles the highest

Contribution by Single authors. Followed by Two authors with 732 (19.5%) and 286 (7.63%) by Unidentified authors respectively.

Degree of authors collaboration is shown in the table no 3:

Various methods have been proposed to calculate the degree of research collaboration. Here in this study the formula proposed by Subramanyam (1983) has been used.

$$C = \frac{Nm}{Nm + Ns}$$

The degree of collaboration

Where,

C=degree of collaboration

Nm= number of multi author

Ns=number of single author

$$C = \frac{1490}{1490 + 2259} = 0.39$$

Thus the degree of collaboration (C) 0.39

So, in the study the degree of collaboration during the overall 10 years (2008-2017) is 0.39.

Table 3. Year-Wise Degree of Collaboration

Year	Single Author(NS)	Multi Authors(NM)	Total (NS+NM)	Degree of Collaboration
2008	343	126	469	0.26
2009	131	92	223	0.41
2010	265	147	412	0.35
2011	136	96	232	0.41
2012	156	120	276	0.43
2013	240	135	375	0.36
2014	332	127	459	0.27
2015	192	143	335	0.42
2016	192	213	405	0.52
2017	271	291	562	0.51
Total	2259	1490	3748	0.39 (Mean)

Table no 3 indicates among the 211 articles published during 2008 to 2017, there were 60.2 % were written by single authors, 39.7 % contributed co-authors, the extent of collaboration was not much popular among the Collection Building, so the Degree of collaboration of authors by year-wise falls between 0.26 and 0.51 with an average of 0.39 during the study period. From 2008 to 2017, it has been increased gradually.

Table 4. Form Wise Distribution of citations

Form	2008	2009	2010	2011	2012	2013	2014	2015	2016	2017	Total	%
Journal	149	120	210	139	149	189	162	230	288	378	2014	53.7
Book	45	12	16	6	30	32	24	21	17	25	228	6.08
Conference	6	7	15	10	5	7	13	5	2	13	83	2.21
Thesis	13	3	4	2	1	2	3	4	7	6	45	1.20
Review	5	-	2	-	7	2	10	7	11	8	52	1.38
Report	11	6	7	4	2	4	8	1	4	3	50	1.33
Bulletin	3	-	3	5	1	7	3	6	5	6	39	1.04
Handbook	1	-	3	-	2	3	-	2	-	2	13	0.34
Chronicle	-	-	-	2	-	-	-	-	-	-	2	0.05
Others	236	75	152	64	79	129	236	59	71	121	1222	32.6
Total	469	223	412	232	276	375	459	335	405	562	3748	100

Table no 4, showed form-wise distribution for citations analysis, out of 3748 citations there are 2014 (53.7%) citations are journals citations. followed by other forms such as books 228 (6.08%), Conference proceedings 83 (2.21%), Thesis 45 (1.20%).

Table 5. Country wise distribution of references

Sr. No	Country	No. of Citations	%	Cumulative	%
1	USA	2741	73.1	2741	4.77
2	India	207	5.52	2948	5.13
3	UK	158	4.21	3106	5.4
4	China	128	3.41	3234	5.63
5	Pakistan	92	2.45	3326	5.79
6	Canada	51	1.36	3377	5.88
7	Nigeria	37	0.98	3414	5.94

8	Malaysia	24	0.64	3438	5.98
9	Africa	20	0.53	3458	60.2
10	Australia	18	0.48	3476	6.05
11	Taiwan	16	0.42	3492	6.08
12	New Zealand	15	0.4	3507	6.1
13	Spain	15	0.4	3522	6.13
14	Netherlands	13	0.34	3535	6.15
15	Singapore	12	0.32	3547	6.17
16	Turkey	11	0.29	3558	6.19
17	Unidentified	190	5.06	3748	100
Total		**3748**	**100**	**57427**	-

Table no. 5 indicates that USA, India, UK, and China have the majority of most cited records 2741 (73.1%); 207 (5.52%); 158 (4.21%) and 128 (3.41%), respectively.

Table 6. Ranked List of Most Cited Journals

Sr.No	Name of the Journal	No. of Citation	Rank No.	%
1	Collection Building	136	1	6.75
2	Journal of Academic Librarianship	72	2	3.57
3	College & Research Libraries	49	3	2.43
4	Library Philosophy and Practice	35	4	1.73
5	Collection Management	34	5	1.68
6	Against the Grain	27	6	1.34
7	Library Hi Tech	24	7	1.19
8	Scientometrics	22	8	1.09
9	The Electronic Library	22	9	1.09
10	Library Journal	20	10	0.99
11	D-Lib Magazine	19	11	0.94
12	Library Trends	18	12	0.89
13	The Serials Librarian	17	13	0.84
14	Library Management	17	14	0.84
15	Library Collections, Acquisitions, and Technical Services	16	15	0.79
16	Journal of American History	14	16	0.69

17	Journal of the Association for History and Computing	14	17	0.69
18	Serials Review	14	18	0.69
19	Journal of Library Administration	13	19	0.64
20	Journal of Librarianship and Information Science	12	20	0.59
21	Libri	12	20	0.59
22	New Library World	12	20	0.59
23	Others	1395	21	67.2
	Total	**2014**	-	**100**

Table No 6 identified a rank list of journals, the study reveals that "Collection Buildinր" scores the 1st rank which account to 136 (6.75%) of the total Citations. "Journal of Academic Librarianship" scored second rank with 72 (3.57%) citations and "College & Research Libraries" 49 (2.43%) scored third rank in the rank list.

Table 7. The Chronological Distribution of Citations

Period	No. of Citation	Cumulative Citation	% of Citations	% of Cumulative Citations
1950 & Before	306	306	8.16	2.88
1951-1960	9	315	0.24	2.97
1961-1970	16	331	0.42	3.12
1971-1980	101	432	2.69	4.07
1981-1990	207	639	5.52	6.02
1991-2000	501	1140	13.3	10.7
2001 & Above	2552	3692	68	34.8
Unidentified	56	3748	1.49	35.3
Total	**3748**	**10603**	**100**	**100**

The study regarding the Ranking of the year-wise citations has been done in order to know the most dominant year. Table 10 gives Ranking of year of distribution of citations which shows that 2552 (34.8%) the highest number of Citations out of a total of 3748 Citations are in year 2001-2018 and lowest number of citations 9 (2.97%) in year 1951-1960. Where it is seen that the researchers cite the latest document. Where it is seen that the researchers cited the highest latest documents 18-20 years (2001 & above).

Table 8. Distribution of E-Citations and P-Citations

Sr. No.	Types of Citation	Citations	%
1	E-Citations	675	18
2	P-Citations	3073	81.9
	Total	**3748**	**100**

Table No. 8. shows that of the total number of 3748 citations, 3073 (81.9%) are printed citations whereas 675 (18 %) are electronic citations, which indicates that the researchers depend mostly on printed literature than the electronic form of literature.

FINDINGS AND CONCLUSION

The findings are based on the analysis of collected data appended in 211 articles and 3748 references in Collection Building.

1. The highest number of references per articles in the year of 2017 with 562 (14.9%) .
2. The single author articles are higher and predomi-nant than multi-author articles.
3. The mean value for the overall and Degree of Collaboration for the year 2008-2017 is found to be 0.39.
4. Out of 3748 citations there are 2014 (53.7%) citations are journals citations.
5. USA, India, and UK, have the majority of most cited records in Collection Building.
6. "Collection Building" ranked as the first most cited 136 (6.75%) journal under the study
7. The study regarding the Ranking of the year of citations

has been done in order to know the most dominant year, found that the researchers cited the highest latest documents (2001 & above).

8. The researchers depend mostly on printed literature

CONCLUSIONS

Citation analysis is a branch of bibliometrics where the unit of analysis is a document that is being cited as a bibliographic reference. The study is based on 3748 references appended to 211 articles from 2008-2017 of Collection Building. It provides the degree of relation between articles, authors, Form Wise Distribution, Country wise distribution, Most Cited Journals, Chronological Distribution of Citations, Distribution of E-Citations and P-Citations etc.

REFERENCES

Collection Building. (n.d). Retrieved from athttps://www.emeraldinsight.com/loi/cb

Nishat, F. (2017). Citation Analysis of Business Research: An International Journal in the Field of Business. DESIDOC Journal of Library & Information Technology, 37(4), 281-286.

Singh, R. K. & Singh, A. P. Dr. (2017). Citation Analysis of International Journal of Library and Information Studies on the Impact Research of Google Scholar: 2011-2015. International Journal of Library and Information Studies, 7(4), 155-161.

Subranmanyam, K. (1983). Bibliometric Studies of Research in Collaboration: A Review. Journal of Information Science, 6(37), 3-8.

Verma, A., Sonker, S. K. & Gupta, V. (2016). A CITATION ANALYSIS OF THE EJOURNAL,

LIBRARY PHILOSOPHY AND PRACTICE (2005-2014). *Library Philosophy and Practice (e-journal)*. Paper 1358. *http://digitalcommons.unl.edu/libphilprac/1358*

4

Content Analysis of Indian Institute of Technology (IIT) Library Websites

Kiran C K
Librarian, MES T O Abdulla Memorial College,
Kunnukara, Ernakulam, Kerala

Archana Unnikrishnan
Asst. Professor, Rajagiri College of Social Sciences (RCSS),
Kalamassery, Ernakulam, Kerala

ABSTRACT

The present study was carried out to analysis the contents available in Indian Institute of Technology library websites. The study mainly focuses on the information available in the library websites like general features, information services, collection details, availability of resources, type of print and non-print materials in the library, OPAC service, Web2.0 applications, etc. For this study the researcher analyzed IIT library websites based on the predetermined criteria's. The same has been analyzed and presented with useful percentage analysis. The suitable tables and graphs have been drawn for presentation of data. The article concluded with findings, suggestions and conclusions.

Keywords : Content analysis, Indian Institute of Technology, Library websites

INTRODUCTION

In the modern world, everything is digitalized and automated. Invention of computer, internet and information technology (IT) are become the milestone in the present century. Information technology makes a great impact on the human beings. Each and every day latest and new technologies are introduced to the world. The latest technologiesPunched cards, typewriters, computers, radio frequency identifier (RFID), biometric gate register etc. are introduced to the academic institutions through the libraries. In the modern era, students get everything from the electronic media. They do not want to waste their time for searching. The information is appeared in front of the users by a simple click. So the number of students visiting the library for information is reduced by the invention of information technology. But the librarians are also moving with the future. Librarians provide all his services through online to the users. The students can access any resources and services of library from where ever he/she like by using a single username and password. Online resources, databases, library websites are make the users comfortable. Library websites are created as part of extension activity of library. But, in this generation library websites are necessary or easy medium to disseminate information to the users. Most of the libraries are evaluated based on the library websites. Library websites provide details about the library resources, services, and facilities. Websites helps to access open source databases, institutional repositories, online database and e-journals, e-books, e-theses, e-dissertations, e-prints and web based reference sources, etc. subscribed by the library. Websites help to computerize the library housekeeping operations.

IMPORTANCE OF STUDY

Websites are considered as the primary source of information. The information in an educational website is mainly utilized by the student community. In the digital environment all the users including students are depends on the information available on the online resources and websites. The students can access library resources with the help of websites in anywhere in India. So the accuracy and relevance of information available in the website should be evaluated. This study tried to evaluate the quality and quantity of the contents in the IIT Library websites.

The Indian Institute of Technology is a group of autonomous engineering and technology oriented institutes of higher education. IIT is the highest education institute in India. The topper most students are admitted to the IIT's through the national level competitive examinations. In digital India information technology, computer and internet are very essential. Most of the students collect data through online resources. The library and library website play a major role in every educational Institutions especially IIT's. Most of the libraries are now becoming automated. The latest and advanced technologies are adopted by the IIT libraries to provide better information to the users.

The study tries to verify and measure the contents, web structure and visibility of the IIT library websites. This study will be useful to librarians and webmasters who are responsible for the development and management of library websites.

OBJECTIVES

This study focuses following objectives:

1. To investigate general information available in the IIT library websites, library services, hyperlinks, to other resources and website aids and tools.
2. To study the URL analysis of IIT library websites.
3. To study the current status of IIT library websites and how they have been integrating contemporary web technologies for library related activities
4. To examine the essential online services available on the IIT Library website.
5. To analyze and compare different IIT library websites which provide web 2.0 applications

METHODOLOGY

The Methodology applied in the present study involves Indian Institute of Technology (IIT) Library website survey and Website content analysis. The investigations in this study consider 23 Indian Institute of Technology (IIT) library websites. For the present study, a checklist was developed for collecting the data. The data is directly collected from the websites in between 21st November 2017 to 28th February 2018.

SCOPE AND LIMITATION OF THE STUDY

The study is confined to examine and explores the contents of Twenty three IIT library websites. The study is limited to the IIT library websites only. No other library websites have been considered for the study. The study focuses only on the content analysis of IIT library websites, and analyses the contents present in the website. The contents of IIT library websites are regularly updated. Internet access facility and computer basic knowledge required to access the websites. Some of the institute doesn't provide the access of library website outside the campus, which is the main limitation faced in the study. The period of data gathering took place from November 2017 to February 2018.

DATA ANALYSIS

This chapter presents analysis and interpretation of data collected from 23 Indian Institute of Technology (IIT) library websites. It is systematically classified and tabulated, analyzed and interpreted. The purpose of the present study is to find out the content analysis of Indian Institute of Technology (IIT) library websites.

IIT's Possessing Library Websites

Table 1 represents the website address of IIT library websites and their domain names. There are 23 Indian Institute of Technology's (IIT) in India. From this 23 only 22 libraries have their own webpage or websites for their libraries. From this 22 library website, six library websites (IIT Hyderabad, IIT Tirupati,

IIT Dhanbad, IIT Bhilai, IIT Dharwad, and IIT Goa) doesn't have sufficient information or they are incomplete in nature. IIT Bhilai library website is under construction work. And IIT Goa library website has only event gallery images. IIT Palakkad library website cannot access from outside the IIT Campus. That website is accessible only inside the campus through IP Address. IIT Jammu library doesn't have any library website or webpage. According to the data, study analyses that there are only 14 library websites/ webpages which are active in nature from the 23 IIT library websites. And the study also shows that only 12 IIT libraries have their own separate library websites. Others have the webpages which is attached to the main official website of IIT.

Table 1. IIT library websites address and domain

	Name of IIT	Short form	URL of library	Domain
1	IIT Kharagpur	IIT KHA	http://www.library.iitkgp.ernet.in/	ernet.in
2	IIT Bombay	IIT BOM	http://www.library.iitb.ac.in/	ac.in
3	IIT Kanpur	IIT KAN	http://pkklib.iitk.ac.in/	ac.in
4	IIT Madras	IIT MAD	http://www.cenlib.iitm.ac.in/	ac.in
5	IIT Delhi	IIT DEL	http://library.iitd.ac.in/	ac.in
6	IIT Guwahati	IIT GUW	http://www.iitg.ernet.in/lib/	ernet.in
7	IIT Roorkee	IIT ROO	http://mgcl.iitr.ac.in/	ac.in
8	IIT Ropar	IIT ROP	http://www.iitrpr.ac.in/library	ac.in
9	IIT Bhubaneswar	IIT BHU	http://library.iitbbs.ac.in/	ac.in
10	IIT Gandhinagar	IIT GAN	https://www.iitgn.ac.in/library.htm	ac.in
11	IIT Hyderabad	IIT HYD	http://library.iith.ac.in/	ac.in
12	IIT Jodhpur	IIT JOD	http://library.iitj.ac.in/	ac.in
13	IIT Patna	IIT PAT	http://library.iitp.ac.in/	ac.in
14	IIT Indore	IIT IND	http://library.iiti.ac.in/	ac.in
15	IIT Mandi	IIT MAN	http://library.iitmandi.ac.in/	ac.in
16	IIT Varanasi	IIT VAR	https://www.iitbhu.ac.in/library/	ac.in
17	IIT Palakkad	IIT PAL	https://iitpkd.ac.in/library	ac.in
18	IIT Tirupati	IIT TIR	http://iittp.ac.in/lib/lib.html	ac.in

19	IIT (ISM) Dhanbad	IIT ISM	http://www.iitismlib.ac.in/	ac.in
20	IIT Bhilai	IIT BHI	https://www.iitbhilai.ac.in/index.php?pid=aca_library	ac.in
21	IIT Goa	IIT GOA	http://www.iitgoa.ac.in/campus.php?area=library	ac.in
22	IIT Jammu	IIT JAM	No	
23	IIT Dharwad	IIT DHA	http://www.iiitdwd.ac.in/library/	ac.in

Provision of Web Domain Analysis

Table 2 reveals that, two types of domain extensions were observed in this study. 87 percent of websites have"ac.in", 9 percent of websites have "ernet.in" and 4 percent of IIT library websites were doesn't have domain extension and web address.

Table 2. Provision of Web Domain Analysis

Domain	No. of institutions
ac.in	20
ernet.in	2

Provision of General Features

Table 3 presents the general features to be included in the library websites. It can be seen from the table that 78.56% of libraries provide the collection details in their library websites/ webpages. 69.56% of libraries provide the contact information. 65.21% libraries provide link to parent organization and details staff's in the websites. 60.86% of libraries provide search facilities and the details about the working hours. 52.17% of libraries contain the details about the memberships. All other features show, below 50% presence in the library websites.

Table 3. Percentage Analysis of general features

	Occurrence (n=23)	Percentage (n=23)
Parent organization	15	65.21%
Aims and Objectives	6	26.08%
Membership	12	52.17%

Working Hours	14	60.86%
Collection details	18	78.56%
Library budget	0	0%
Staff details	15	65.21%
User Orientation/ directions	9	39.13%
FAQ	7	30.43%
Location	7	30.43%
Contact information	16	69.56%
Search facilities	14	60.86%

Provision of Library Section Information

Table 4 analyzes the occurrence of sections in the library websites. But most of the library websites doesn't provide much detail about the library sections through the websites. 60.86% of library websites shows circulation details in the websites. Other section details are not given by the libraries. Only 6 library websites provide the information about acquisition section (26.08%) technical section (26.08%) and journal section. Only 5 libraries provide the information about the digital library (21.73%). The details about the maintenance section (8.69%) are very rare. Only 2 libraries provide the maintenance details.

Table 4. Percentage analysis of library sections

	Occurrence(n=23)	Percentage(n=23)
Acquisition	6	26.08%
Technical section	6	26.08%
Circulation	14	60.86%
Journal section	6	26.08%
Digital library	5	21.73%
Maintenance	2	8.69%

Provision of Print Collections

Table 5 shows that most of the 15 IIT library websites provide the details about the books (65.21%). 16 IIT library websites provide the details of journals (69.56%). 10 IIT library websites provide the details of thesis (43.47%). 8 IIT library websites (34.78%) provide the details of magazines and CD/DVD's. The collection details of bound volumes (26.08%), newspaper (17.39%), audio/video (8.69%), standards (8.69%), microforms (8.69%) are very rarely available on the sites.

Table 5. Percentage analysis of print collections

	Occurrence(n=23)	Percentage(n=23)
Books	15	65.21%
Journals	16	69.56%
Magazine	8	34.78%
Thesis	10	43.47%
Bound Volumes	6	26.08%
Newspaper	4	17.39%
CD/DVD	8	34.78%
Audio/ Video	2	8.69%
Standards	2	8.69%
Microforms	2	8.69%

Provision of Databases and E-Resources Information

Table 6 provides information about the percentage of each e- resource available in IIT library websites. By analyzing the table, it is shows that 19 library websites (82.60%) provide the information about the e-journals and 16 libraries provides information about e-databases and e- books (69.56%). And the details about e-thesis (30.43%) and e-standards (30.43%) are rarely available on the library websites. Through the study it is very noted that only 14 library has institutional digital repository (60.86%).

Table 6. Percentage analysis of databases and e-resources

	Occurrence (n=23)	Percentage (n=23)
E-journals	19	82.60%
E-databases	16	69.56%
E-books	16	69.56%

E-thesis	7	30.43%
E-standards	7	30.43%
Open access resources	13	56.52%
Bibliographic databases	13	56.52%
Institutional Digital Repository	14	60.86%

Provision of Information Services

Table 7 represents the information services provided by the IIT libraries. 56.52% of libraries provide new arrival facility in the libraries. 47.82% of libraries provide inter library loan facility. 43.47% libraries provide the faculty and in house publication details in their websites. Other information services are shows below 40% only.

Table 7. Percentage analysis of information services

	Occurrence (n=23)	Percentage (n=23)
New Arrivals	13	56.52%
Online reservation	4	17.39%
Publications	10	43.47%
Intranet implementation	8	34.78%
Ask a Librarian	6	26.08%
Inter Library Loan	11	47.82%
Document Delivery Service	5	21.73%
Book Bank	7	30.43%
Reference Service	9	39.13%
Reprography	8	34.78%
Remote access	6	26.08%
CAS	2	8.69%
E-Mail Alert	3	13.04%

OPAC and Web OPAC

Table 8 shows that only 18 library websites have their own OPAC (78.26%) facility. And only five library websites provide the Web OPAC services. It is also noted that, other five library websites provide wrong information about web OPAC in their library website. These websites provide the information that they are providing Web OPAC service. But by the content analysis it is analyzed that these libraries doesn't provide Web OPAC service. They provide only OPAC service.

Table 8. Percentage analysis of OPAC and Web OPAC

	Occurrence (n=23)	Percentage (n=23)
OPAC	18	78.26%
Web OPAC	5	21.74%
No OPAC	5	21.74%

Web 2.0 Applications

Table 9 shows that the web2.0 applications of IIT libraries are not efficient. Six library websites provide the Facebook (26.08%) option in their websites. Five library websites provide Twitter (21.73%), four library websites provide the link to YouTube (17.39%), two library websites provide link to Instagram and RSS Feed (8.69%).And only one library website provides the links to Blog and Pinterest (4.34%).

Table 9. Percentage analysis of web 2.0 applications

	Occurrence (n=23)	Percentage (n=23)
Blog	1	4.34%
RSS Feed	2	8.69%
Facebook	6	26.08%
Twitter	5	21.73%
YouTube	4	17.39%
Flicker	0	0%
Instagram	2	8.69%
Pinterest	1	4.34%

FINDINGS

- Only 22 IIT libraries have their own webpages or websites. Only 14 IIT library websites/ webpages are active in nature. Only 12 IIT library websites have their own separate library websites. Others have the webpages which are attached to the main official IIT library websites.

- Majority of library websites possess "ac.in" domain name. A few of library websites possess "ernet.in" domain name in their website address. A limited number of library websites doesn't have domain address.
- The general features of library websites doesn't followed in most of the IIT library websites.
- Only 21.73% of libraries are digital libraries.
- IIT's provide only very few information services.
- Link to e-journals was found 82.60% of the library websites.
- Only 60.86% libraries provide institutional digital repositories.
- The libraries give details about the collections like books, magazines, journals, bound volumes and newspapers. Other information resources like CD, DVD, Audio visual aids details are not available on the websites.
- Only 78.26% libraries provide the Web OPAC service.
- Facebook, Twitter and YouTube are the commonly used web 2.0 applications in IIT library websites.

SUGGESTIONS AND CONCLUSION

- All the IIT libraries should develop their own separate library websites with registered domain address. Because it disseminate knowledge and information among users and attracts potential users by showing richness of collection/ resources, variety of services, number of facilities, etc.
- The library websites should be attractive and user friendly
- Suggest to providing adequate information in library websites of IIT Hyderabad, IIT Tirupati, IIT Dhanbad, IIT Bhilai, IIT Dharwad, IIT Goa. Because they doesn't have sufficient information regarding library.
- The webmasters should add minimum required information

about the library in the website.

- The information present in the websites should be regularly updated and Error Free.
- All IIT libraries should initiate digital library project.
- All the IIT libraries should implement Web OPAC Service to the users which enhance usage of libraries.
- Online circulation system should be started in IIT libraries.
- All the Library Websites must provide details regarding collection, services and Facilities which is helpful to the users.
- The presence of Frequently Asked Questions (FAQ's) helps the users to solve their doubts about the services and facilities present in the library.
- Include location facility which helps the outside users to find out the location of library and parent organization
- Library staffs are the major part of the library. So the details about staff name, photograph and Designations etc. to be included in the library website.
- The contact details help the users to contact the library and librarian. But most of IIT's doesn't provide sufficient information in their websites
- The library website should add more useful out links to other resources.
- The web 2.0 technologies should be completely adapted to the IIT libraries.
- Incomplete in links and out links in the library website should be avoided which may mislead the users.
- All the IIT libraries need an out link to the parent organization, which emphasizes the authencity of the websites.
- The information services like Ask A Librarian, Document Delivery Service (DDS), Inter Library Loan (ILL), Book bank

facility, reference services and reprographic services should be need more attention in IIT's.

- All the IIT libraries should implement email alert service. The e-mail alert service helps the users to be alert about the latest information in the library.
- The webmaster details should be inserted in the library websites. Those help the users to discuss the website feedback, directly with the webmaster.
- The library websites doesn't provide any details about the library budgets. The details about the library budget to be included in the website.
- The faculty publication and institution publication details are helps the users to analyze the standard of the IIT's.
- The intranet implementation details to be included in the website.

REFERENCE

1. Kiran Kumar, G., Kumbar, M., &Somashekara, Y. L. (2012). Content Analysis of Indian Institutes of Technology Library Websites (pp. 484–492). Presented at the Empowering Libraries for Lifelong Learning Skills (Excellence, Creativity and Challenges), Agra.
2. Madhusudhan, M (2012). Content Evaluation of Indian Institutes of Technology Library Websites in India.*World Digital Libraries: An International Journal, 5*(2). https://doi.org/10.3233/WDL-120087
3. Vijayakumar, M., Kannappanavar, B U., and Mestri, M. 2009. "Content analysis of Indian Institutes of Technology libraries web portals: A study. *DESIDOC Journal of Library and Information Technology* 29(1): 57–63.
4. http://www.library.iitkgp.ernet.in/
5. http://www.library.iitb.ac.in/
6. http://pkklib.iitk.ac.in/
7. http://www.cenlib.iitm.ac.in/
8. http://library.iitd.ac.in/
9. http://www.iitg.ernet.in/lib/
10. http://mgcl.iitr.ac.in/
11. http://www.iitrpr.ac.in/library

12. http://library.iitbbs.ac.in/
13. https://www.iitgn.ac.in/library.htm
14. http://library.iith.ac.in/
15. http://library.iitj.ac.in/
16. http://library.iitp.ac.in/
17. http://library.iiti.ac.in/
18. http://library.iitmandi.ac.in/
19. https://www.iitbhu.ac.in/library/
20. https://iitpkd.ac.in/library
21. http://iittp.ac.in/lib/lib.html
22. http://www.iitismlib.ac.in/
23. https://www.iitbhilai.ac.in/index.php?pid=aca_library
24. http://www.iitgoa.ac.in/campus.php?area=library
25. http://www.iiitdwd.ac.in/library/

5

e-PG Pathshala, An Indian Based E-learning Source : A Quantitative Analysis

Hauminlun
Research Scholar, University of Delhi

ABSTRACT

An open access e-learning source is a current trend which has been used by many educators and learners. It is an opportunity for someone who cannot afford quality education. The e-PG Pathshala is a e-learning source, joint initiative of Ministry of Human Resource Development (MHRD), Govt. of India and National Council of Educational Research and Training (NCERT) that developed showcasing and disseminating all educational e-resources including textbooks, audio, video, periodicals, and a variety of other print and non-print materials for Students, Teachers, Parents, researchers and educators. Educators can extend teaching material outside of the class rooms and facilitate the students with a handy teaching material. The present study attempted to deliver the quantitative analysis of one of the most important Indian based e-learning source –e-PG Pathshala.

Keywords: e-learning, e-PG Pathshala, CD-ROM, Module,web-based

1. INTRODUCTION

The evolution of information and technology these past few decades have been staggeringly fast. Such advance changes ultimately demand for the changes in the pattern of the teaching and learning. The education system has also been in constant shift in delivering contents to the pupils. Consequently, modern technology also helps in paradigm shift from the conventional classroom teaching methods adopted in the past to non-conventional teaching aids so as to encourage interactive forms of learning in students through active participation and integrative reasoning where the relationship of the teacher and the taught has undergone tremendous transformation. "Some of the nonconventional teaching methods adopted are learning through active participation by the students through computer-assisted learning (CD-ROMs), Web based learning (undergraduate projects), e-learning, virtual laboratories, seminars, audiovisual aids (video-based demonstrations) and so on (9).

2. E-LEARNING

The mode of education until the early '00s was in classroom which involves students with a teacher who led the process. It is where Physical presence was a no-brainer, and there were no other method that classroom teaching. Then the computer evolution happened and it radically changed the learning landscape.(20)

The term e-learning was first used in the professional environment in the year 1999 at CBT Seminar at Los Angeles. E-learning is essentially imparting education through computer and network enabled digital technologies which include among other things, internet, intranet, computer, satellite TV, CDROM, audio and video resources. Therefore e-learning could be broadly defined as use of Information and Communication Technology (ICT) to enhance and support learning. This could range from teachers and students using e-mail for communication to entirely online courses. This term is used synonymously with virtual learning, online learning, computer based learning, web based learning, and networked learning. Whatever may be the definition of e-learning, it is currently changing the way schools and colleges teach and the students learn (21).E-Learning has many interpretations but in short it stands for learning by electronic means. This means learning not directly from lecture notes, books or face-to-face from teacher. Common forms are computer-based training and web based lessons or on-line lessons.

3. DEFINITION

There can be a different ways of defining E-learning.

Rosenberg : "E-learning refers to the use of Internet technologies to deliver a broad array of solutions that enhance knowledge and performance." Rosenberg claims that e-learning is based on three fundamental criteria:

i. E-learning is networked, instant updating, storage and retrieval, distribution and sharing of information is therefore possible.

ii. E-learning is delivered to the end-user via a computer using standard internet technologies.

iii. E-learning focuses on the broadest view of learning: Learning solutions going beyond the traditional paradigms of training.

iv. E-learning involves the use of a computer or electronic device (e.g. a mobile phone) in some way to provide training, educational or learning material. (22)

According to The Economic Times, eLearning is defined as learning system based on formalised teaching but with the help of electronic resources is known as E-learning.(25)

"E-learning refers to educational processes that utilise information and communications technology to mediate synchronous as well as asynchronous learning and teaching activities" (8)

4. BENEFITS OF E-LEARNING

The benefits of e-learning are as follow:

i. Multiple Delivery Options : Easy delivery of information to multiple users and students by deploying any options like internet, intranet and CD ROM.

ii. Just-in-Time Training : E-Learning is easily accessible to employees and students. It is accessible at any time and there is no waiting for classes.

iii. Engaging and Effective : It is the combination of audio, animation and software simulations that produce highly engaging multimedia training. Courses today use realistic simulations, hands-on exercises, and role-playing scenarios to help employees "learn while doing".

iv. Assessment : Student assessment can be a powerful and helpful aid in the learning process. With many E-Learning products, pre-assessments are available to determine which topics students are already familiar with so that they can focus on key areas where they need help.

v. Increased Productivity : Training is a proven benefit and incentive to employees, giving them the opportunity to advance their skills and careers.

vi. Lower Cost : E-Learning is available at a fraction of the cost of classroom learning and is provided right to student's desktops, eliminating the need for travel and expense (2).

5. REVIEW OF RELATED LITERATURE:

E-leaning is mostly famous for its web based, fast delivery and own paced learning. Stojanovic (2001) discussed eLearning is fast, relevant and just-in-time learning grown from the learning requirements of the new, dynamically changing, distributed business world. Rosenberg (2001) discussed that internet and intranet technologies offer tremendous opportunities to bring learning into the mainstream of business. Welsh, Elizabeth T., et al. (2003) pointed out that the use of network technology to deliver training is the latest trend in the training and development industry and has been heralded as the 'e-learning revolution.'

Zhang (2004) pointed out that an e-learning environment that emphasizes learner-cantered activity and system interactivity, remote learners can outperform traditional classroom students.

Sener (2015) has pointed out that e-learning has evolved into a global change agent in higher education and evolved as the primary form of distance education, also transforming instruction on campus.

Tyler-Smith, K. (2006) found that eLearners often experience cognitive overload, in the early stages of an online course and it is suggested that this is a likely contributor to high dropout rates, particularly in terms of those withdrawing within the first few weeks of the course start

Choules, A. P. (2007) discussed that electronic learning (elearning) is moving from textbooks in electronic format to a truly interactive medium that can be delivered to meet the educational needs of students and postgraduate learners.

Mahmoud M. El-Khouly (2008) pointed out that in order to provide education to the growing population with quality, accessible, and numerous educational opportunities, both the government and the private sector CD-rom plays an important role. Although internet are hand and widely available the CD_ROM offers a better options for e-learning.

Martínez-Torres, M., Toral, S., & Barrero, F. (2011) The widespread availability of digital learning resources in a variety of media formats has promoted the proliferation of eLearning systems as an integral part of teaching across all sectors of education.

Aparicio (2013) discussed that E-learning systems are widely used from academia to industry and it raises new research contexts. The author also pointed out that elearning E-learning systems play a significant role in the learning activities and consist of multiple collaborative learning systems were implemented to improve people interaction, communication, working, coordinating activities, socializing and learning.

Harandi, S. R. (2015) found that E-learning has a significant role in instruction of students in higher education and confirmed that e-learning is an element which affects students' motivation.

Makkar, L., Alsadoon, A., Prasad, P., & Elchouemi, A. (2016) discussed that E-Learning has become an important means of gaining education/knowledge with the help of electronic media, typically on the Internet. The authors also found that the majority of the students had positive perceptions of the proposed model with regard to its impact on student's academic performance.

Despite its advantages, eLearning also has some drawback. Sun (2008), E-learning is emerging as the new paradigm of modern education. Worldwide, the e-learning market has a growth rate of 35.6%, but failures exist. "The systems are rarely planned in advance taking into account its final usefulness. At most, they are validated through learner experience using the final implemented system" (Martínez-Torres, M., Toral, S., & Barrero, F., 2011).

6. E-PG PATHSHALA

The digital India campaign has promoted extensive use of ICTs in the teaching and learning. e-PG Pathshala is one portal under which high quality, curriculum based, interactive content in different subjects across all disciplines of social sciences, arts, fine arts and humanities, natural and mathematical sciences, linguistics and languages is being developed. MHRD, under its national mission on education through ICT (NME-ICT), has assigned work to the UGC for development of e-content in 68 subjects at post graduate level. The content and its quality is the key component of education system.

The e-PG Pathshala, a joint initiative of Ministry of Human Resource Development (MHRD), Govt. of India and National Council of Educational Research and Training (NCERT) has been developed for showcasing and disseminating all educational e-resources including textbooks, audio, video, periodicals, and a variety of other print and non-print materials for Students, Teachers, Parents, researchers and educators. It provides access to digital textbooks for all classes, graded learning materials and enables participation in exhibitions, contests, festivals, workshops, etc. (23)

The content and its quality is the key component of education system. An e-PG Pathshala Project has been launched by the UGC. The project will standardize textbook materials for MA, MSc and MCom courses in different universities and the first national level meeting of the coordinators and authors of different subjects was convened in New Delhi.

8. CONTENT OF E-PG PATHSHALA

E-Content developed under Four Quadrant Approach. It is required to develop e-content in four quadrants, as recommended by the MHRD. The quadrants are as under:

i. First Quadrant : Textual Document, PDF / e-Books / illustration, documents & Interactivity wherever required Simulations, Virtual Labs.

ii. Second Quadrant : Video and Audio Content in an organised form, Animation.

iii. Third Quadrant : MCQ, Problems, Quizzes, Assignments, & solutions, online feedback through discuss forums & setting up the FAZ, Clarifications on general misconceptions etc.

iv. Fourth Quadrant : Related Links, Wikipedia Development of Course, Open content on Internet, Cases Studies, Anecdotal information, Historical development of the subject, Articles.

9. OBJECTIVES

The objectives of e-PG Pathshala are:

i. Major objective of this e-PG Pathshala is to develop holistic e-content for postgraduate students with an aim to benefit the learners beyond syllabi.

ii. Develop e-content in 77 subjects at postgraduate. Impart training to subject experts in the process of e-content creation;

iii. Make e-content available to students and peers using different delivery modes to impart formal and informal education and for supplementing and complementing the process of teaching and learning in higher education; Make these e-content available for open access.

iv. Drawing expert from different subject and from different levels i.e. colleges, universities and R & D laboratories to create and uploading study materials in the form of text and videos.

v. Promote usage of e-content amongst students and peer;

vi. To develop e-content in all post graduate courses drawing expertise from subject experts of Colleges, Universities and R&D laboratories.

10. QUANTITATIVE ANALYSIS OF E-PG PATHSHALA

Quantitative analysis is based on describing and interpreting objects statistically and with numbers. It aims to interprete the data collected for the phenomenon through numeric variables and statistics (https://koppa.jyu.fi/avoimet/hum/menetelmapolkuja/en/methodmap/data-analysis/quantitative-analysis). The statistical we will take into account here includes the number of subject categories, number of visitors; total number of document available etc. let us look upon them one by one:

i. Subject Categories

The resources provided by e-PG Pathshala are 7 in subject categories. The Subject categories have different areas of study and 72 subjects are provided by ePG Pathshala.

The following Chart shows the graphical representation of the above data.

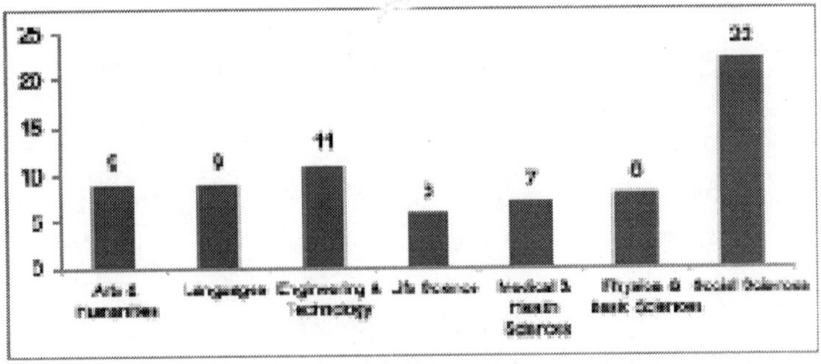

Fig. 1. Subject categories and No. of Subjects.

The above chart shows the number of subject and subject categories. The Social Science category has the highest number of subject i.e. 22 followed by engineering and technology with 11 subject and life science category stand at the least with just 6 subjects.

ii. Content of e-PG Pathshala

The content e-PG Pathshala consist of content of document like, e-text, video, quiz and Module for the subject.

Table 1. Content of e-PG Pathshala

Sl.No	Content	No. of Content
1	Module	18000+
2	Subjects	7
3	Total Paper	723
4	e-Text	20000+
5	Video	19000+
6	Experts	3200 +
7	Quiz	30000+

iii. Subjects and Total no. of Modules

While the total subject are divided into 7 different categories, the different categories further consist of 67 different subjects and the subject are further have numbers of document.

Table 2. Showing total subjects and total no. of Document content

Sl. No	Subject	Modules
1	Adult Education	189
2	Analytical Chemistry/Instrumentation	162
3	Anthropology	533
4	Architecture	160
5	Biochemistry	254
7	Biophysics	169
8	Biotechnology	214
9	Botany	116
10	Buddhist Studies	28
11	Business Economics	457
12	Chemistry	454
13	Chinese	26
14	Commerce	468
15	Comparative Study of Religions	69
16	Computer Science	463
17	Criminology	466
18	Earth Sciences	27
19	Economics	537
20	Education	51
21	Electronic Science	85
22	English	558
23	Environmental Sciences	111
24	Food and Nutrition	184
25	Food Technology	172
26	Forensic Science	557
27	Geography	299
28	Geology	135
29	Hindi	583
30	Home Science	193
31	Hotel and tourism Management	249
32	Human Resource Management	599

33	Human Rights and Duties	206
34	Indian Culture	523
35	Information Technology	288
36	Japanese	278
37	Jyotish- ganit	331
38	Law	461
39	Library and Information Science	343
40	Linguistics	279
41	M Plannning	0
42	Management	590
43	Material Science	81
44	Mathematics	486
45	Media and communication	376
46	Performing Arts(Dance/Drama/Theatre)	559
47	Pharmaceutical Science	37
48	Philosophy	144
49	Physical Education, Sports and Health Education	36
50	Physics	171
51	Political Science	189
52	Population Studies	357
53	Psychology	596
54	Public Administration	189
55	Risk / Disaster Management	16
56	Russian Studies	422
57	Sanskrit (Acharya in Vyakrana)	533
58	Sanskrit (M.A)	634
59	Social Medicine and Community Health	90
60	Social Work Education	424
61	Sociology	630
62	Spanish	560
63	Statistics	506
64	Urdu	158
65	Visual Arts	244
66	Women Studies/Gender Studies	105
67	Zoology	174
	Total	**19584**

Table 3 shows that the subject Sanskrit (M.A) has the highest number of modules with 634 which is followed by sociology (630). There are also subject like Jyotish- ganit which has 331 and Mplanning which has no module at all.

iv. Visitor

The e-PG Pathshala has a good numbers of visitors throughout the year round. The following information provides the number of visitors from different states, so far from the day it was created.

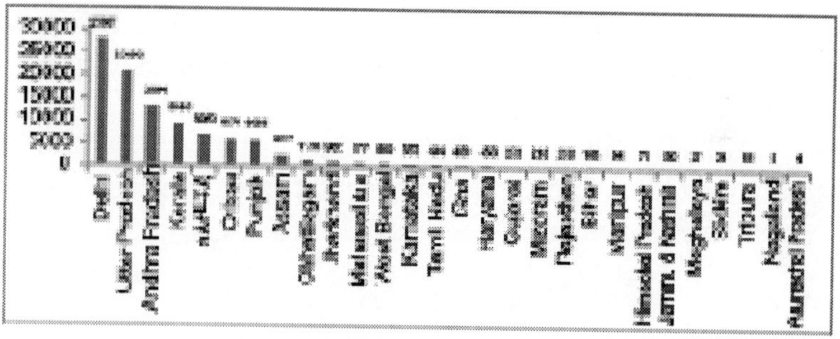

Fig. 2. State wise visitor of e-PG Pathshala

Figure 2 show the number of visitors of e-PG Pathshala from different states. Delhi has the largest number of vistor to e-PG Pathshala with 271862 visitor so far. Delhi is followed by Uttar Pradesh (20896), Andhra Pradesh (13064) and kerala (9540). On the other end the least visitor includes Arunachal Pradesh with 4 visitor so far which is closely followed by Nagaland with just 9 visitors.

v. Registered Users

The following information provides the number of registered users per month for the since it was e-PG Pathshala was introduced. The information are as follow:

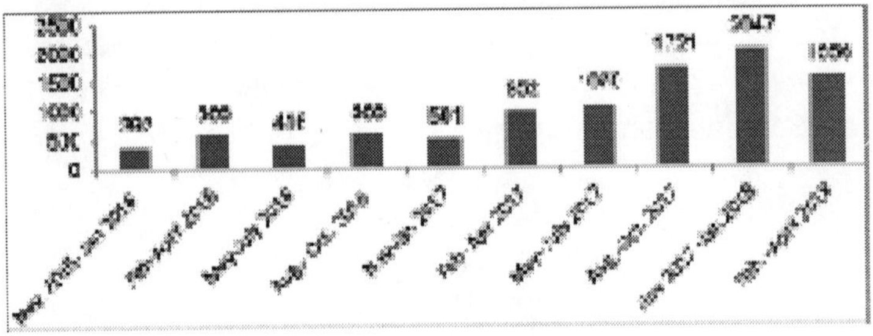

Fig. 3. Registered users

The chart shows the total registration of the past 21 months taking it to account of 3 month each, form 2015 Nov to April 2018. The trends of registration fluctuate a lot and surprisingly November 2017 to January 2018 has the largest share of registration within the given time which is followed by August to October 2017. Overall the numbers of new registration have increased as we move on.

vi. Subject wise Visitors

User used the information source according to their need. Each subject has different amount of users. The following figure shows how information is used by different users based on subject.

Table 3. Subject wise Visitors

Sl.No	Subject	Number of visitors
1	Library and Information Science	475227
2	Anthropology	175493
3	English	172461
4	Chemistry	165477
5	economics	126336
6	Commerce	109037
7	Law	95679
8	Hindi	87623
9	Sociology	82913
10	Mathematics	81772

Table 3 shows that library and information science has the latgest number of visitors(475227) so far, which is followed by anthropology with (175493 visitors) which is closely followed by English (172461).

vii. Module Uploaded

Every subject has different numbers of module uploaded. The following figure show the number of module uploaded per subject.

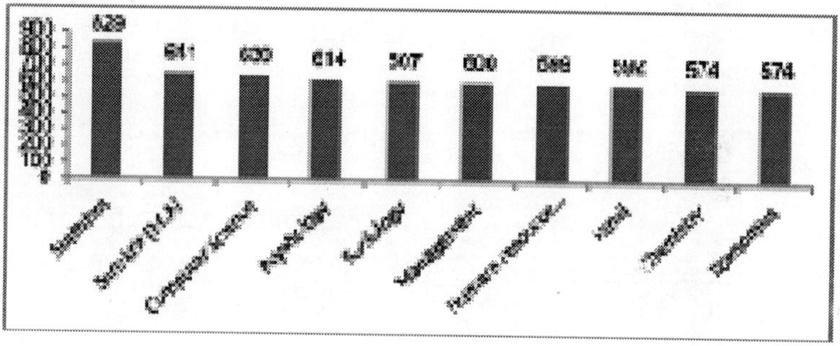

Fig. 4. Module Uploaded

FINDINGS AND CONCLUSION

The present study found that:

a. e-PG Pathshala is a free learning source which is accessible by anyone and it so far has 67 subject listed in the site.

b. Social science has the largest number of subject uploaded which is followed by engineering and technology. This could be due to the fact that social science has a wide variety of subjects and there are large number of creators and users too.

c. Delhi, U.P and Andhra Pradesh have the highest visitor throughout the country and states like Arunachal Pradesh and Nagaland has the lowest visitor. This could be due to the lack awareness about the availability of e-learning source. Other reason could be the non-availability or expensive infrastructure. Though the access to the course is 100% free there is a large amount of money to invest in devices and internet connection.

d. Registration to ePG Pathshala fluctuates a lot, but has a steady increase in number of registered users. Surprisingly the month from November 2017 to January 2018 has the largest share of registration within the given time.

e. There are thousands of visitor to different subject. Library and information science has the largest number of visitors (475227) so far, which is followed by anthropology with (175493 visitors) which is closely followed by English (172461).

f. Stataistic, Sanskrit and computer science has the highest number of modules.

e-PG Pathshala is an opportunity for someone who cannot pay quality education. Educators can extend teaching material outside of the class rooms and facilitate the students with a handy teaching material. The present study shows that there are large numbers of information and document available in the form of video&audio and text. The e PG pathshala is well maintained and easy to access in finding information where one can find their desire information through different module. There is also some lack of awareness of the courses to different potential users as some states has like Arunachal and Nagaland has a one digit visitor. Awareness of the eLearning source and the step involved to access is another areas to take care of for the further success of e-PG Pathshala.

REFERENCES

1. Aparicio, M., & Bacao, F. (2013). E-learning concept trends. *Proceedings of the 2013 International Conference on Information Systems and Design of Communication - ISDOC 13*. doi:10.1145/2503859.2503872

2. Bhandari, R. (2015). Making Distance Learning Effective: A New Approach in Maritime Education & Training. Retrieved May 10, 2018, from https://www.sp.edu.sg/wps/wcm/connect/e49482804f5b9c3caf97af67a2a3b15c/distlearn.pdf?MOD=AJPERES& attachment=true&id=1251367235991

3. Choules, A. P. (2007). The use of elearning in medical education: A review of the current situation. Postgraduate Medical Journal, 83(978), 212-216. doi:10.1136/pgmj.2006.054189

4. El-Khouly, Mahmoud M. "CD-ROM Use in e-Learning." CD-ROM Use in e-Learning, www.eurodl.org/materials/contrib/2008/El-Khouly.htm. Accessed 20 July 2017.

5. e-PG Pathshala Project by UGC for PG Subjects, *www.edu-leaders.com/articles/19021/e-pg-pathshala-project-by-ugc-for-pg-subjects. Accessed 21 July 2017*

6. Harandi, S. R. (2015). Effects of e-learning on Students' Motivation. Procedia - Social and Behavioral Sciences, 181, 423-430. doi:10.1016/j.sbspro.2015.04.905

7. Hajam, Manzoor Ahmad. SWOT ANALYSIS OF E-PG PATHSHALA. www.researchgate.net/profile/Manzoor_Hajam2/publication/318108077_SWOT_ANALYSIS_OF_E-PG_PATHSHALA/links/595dbe500f7e9b3aefadfdd7/SWOT-ANALYSIS-OF-E-PG-PATHSHALA. Accessed 21 July 2017.

8. Jereb, E., & Šmitek, B. (2006). Applying multimedia instruction in e learning. *Innovations in Education and Teaching International,43*(1), 15-27. doi:10.1080/14703290500467335

9. Kumari, N. Kalpana. "Modern and innovative practices and impact on teacher education." *learning* 1.2 (2012). http://www.ijmer.in/pdf/volume1-issue2-2012/430-435.pdf

10. Makkar, L., Alsadoon, A., Prasad, P., & Elchouemi, A. (2016). Impact of e-Learning on students: A proposal and evaluation of enhanced e-learning model to increase the academic performance of university students. 2016 Sixth International Conference on Digital Information Processing and Communications (ICDIPC). doi:10.1109/icdipc.2016.7470797

11. Martínez-Torres, M., Toral, S., & Barrero, F. (2011). Identification of the design variables of eLearning tools. Interacting with Computers, 23(3), 279-288. doi:10.1016/j.intcom.2011.04.004

12. Rosenberg, M. J. (2001). E-Learning: Strategies for Delivering Knowledge in the Digital Age (McGraw-Hill) doi:. Retrieved May 9, 2018, from http://doi.contentdirections.com/mr/mgh.jsp?doi=10.1036/0071362681

13. Stojanovic, L., Staab, S., & Studer, R. (2001). eLearning based on the Semantic Web. In *WebNet2001-World Conference on the WWW and Internet* (pp. 23-27). https://pdfs.semanticscholar.org/7742/06a4592d12c246e809546775fd5437e9ee13.pdf

14. Sener, J. (2015, August 17). E-Learning Definitions. Retrieved May 9, 2018, from https://onlinelearningconsortium.org/updated-e-learning-definitions-2/

15. Sun, Pei-Chen.et.al "What Drives a Successful e-Learning? An Empirical Investigation of the Critical Factors Influencing Learner Satisfaction." - ScienceDirect, 2008, www.sciencedirect.com/science/article/pii/S0360131506001874. Accessed 22 July 2017.

16. Tyler-Smith, K. (2006). Early attrition among first time eLearners: A review of factors that contribute to drop-out, withdrawal and non-completion rates of adult learners undertaking eLearning programmes. *Journal of Online learning and Teaching, 2*(2), 73-85. http://jolt.merlot.org/vol2no2/tyler-smith.htm.

17. Welsh, E. T., Wanberg, C. R., Brown, K. G., & Simmering, M. J. (2003). E-learning: Emerging uses, empirical results and future directions. International Journal of Training and Development, 7(4), 245-258. doi:10.1046/j.1360-3736.2003.00184.x

18. Zhang, Dongsong .et.al. "Can e-Learning Replace Classroom Learning?" Communications of the ACM, ACM, 2004, dl.acm.org/citation.cfm?id=986216. Accessed 22 July 2017.

19. http://epgp.inflibnet.ac.in/stats/home.php

20. https://www.talentlms.com/elearning/elearning-101-jan2014-v1.1.pdf

21. http://www.riemysore.ac.in/ict/unit__7__elearning.html

22. http://www.nwlink.com/~donclark/hrd/elearning/define.html

23. http://vikaspedia.in/education/interactive-resources/e-pathshala

24. https://koppa.jyu.fi/avoimet/hum/menetelmapolkuja/en/methodmap/data-analysis/quantitative-analysis

25. https://economictimes.indiatimes.com/definition/e-learning

6

Influence of Internet on Agricultural Extension Practitioners for Farm Advisory Services: A Case Study of Uttar Banga Krishi Vishwavidyalaya, West Bengal

Santanu Das
Librarian, Surya Sen College
Siliguri, West Bengal, Pin- 734004

ABSTRACT

India has been experiencing major changes in agricultural extension system since the beginning of the 21st century. Internet, the base of IT, overcomes some of these most challenging issues relating to advisory services like – accessibility, literacy and language barriers, geographic coverage and local focus. The Internet can play a vital role in this kind of new and fast changing agricultural extension system. Keeping the above fact in mind, the research was conducted with the objectives, like to study the accessibility of Internet services among university extension personnel, to study the impact of Internet on Farm advisory services and to ascertain the constraints perceived in receiving of Internet services. The present study was conducted at Uttar Banga Krishi Vishwavidyalaya (UBKV). In this research, census survey of total 76 extension personnel was adopted with help of a specially designed questionnaire. Out of total 76 extension personnel, 71 had responded timely and positively with overall response rate being 93.42 per cent.

Keywords : Extension Practitioner, Agricultural Extension Service, Farm Advisory Service, Internet, ICT

1. INTRODUCTION

India is one of the developing countries located in the South-West Asia region of Asia Continent. Because of its ever-growing population, India is currently estimated to be more than 1.26 billion people, the second highly populated country in Asia next to China. Indian economy, like most developing countries, is based on agriculture. Economy of India is the tenth-largest in the world by nominal GDP and the third-largest by Purchasing Power Parity (PPP). The country is one of the G-20 major economies, a member of BRICS and a developing economy that is among the top 20 global traders according to the WTO. 70 per cent of the population in India lives in rural areas, engaged in agrarian economy with agriculture and allied sectors employing 51 per cent of the total workforce but accounting for only 17 per cent of the GDP. Without rural development India cannot optimally realize its growth potential and claim its place in the world. It is very vital to engage farmers, large enough to adopt newly-generated technologies and produce significant marketed surpluses that will improve their living standards.

21st century would be widely acclaimed as the era of Information Technology (IT) for India and most of the developing world. This was the time when the Information Technology started making inroad into the hitherto unreached countries in a big way. India has been experiencing major changes in agricultural extension system since the beginning of the 21st century. The reform included both demand and supply side measures. Information and Communication Technology (ICT) has great potential to revamp agricultural extension in a big way. Until ICTs offered farmers a channel for communicating directly with distant technicians and experts, many farmers could wait months or years for an extension workers to provide technical advice, and often that advice did not address immediate concerns. Communication has always been the most important ingredient of human existence on the earth. Importance of communication in socialization has been widely acknowledged by the social science researchers. In fact, both are the two sides of the same coin. Quick communication is the essence of modern civilization (Adejo & Haruna, 2009).

E-Agriculture is an emerging field focusing on the enhancement of agricultural and rural development through improved information and communication processes. More specifically, e-Agriculture involves the conceptualization, design, development, evaluation and application of innovative ways to use internet in the rural domain, with a primary focus on agriculture. E-Agriculture is a relatively new term and we fully expect its scope to change and evolve as our understanding of the area grows. Private sector initiatives like contract farming have commercialized the Indian agricultural sector. All stakeholders of agriculture sector need information and knowledge about these phases to manage them efficiently.

The main applications of internet in agricultural sector are: Office Automation, Wireless Technologies, Geographic Information Systems (GIS), Computer-Controlled Devices (automated systems), Smartphone Mobile Apps in Agriculture, Radio-Frequency Identification Technology (RFID), and Agricultural Resources and Services Management (ARSM). The important agricultural portals for agricultural development are: Haritgyan.com, TOEHOLDINDIA.com, ITC's Soyachoupal.com,

Plantersnet.com, Krishnworld.net, Agriwatch.com, Acquachoupal.com, Fertindia.com, Indiaagrisat.com, Indiancommodities.com, Fci.web.in, etc. Some initiatives in India that use internet for agricultural development are: National Agriculture Technology Project, AGMARKNET, Community Information Centres and Warana Wired Village Project by Government of India. Similarly, state governments have also taken initiatives to use internet in various agricultural projects like, Janmithra (Rajasthan), Gyandoot (Madhya Pradesh), e-Seva (Andhra Pradesh) Bhoomi (Land Record Computerization), Raitha Samparka Kendra Online (Karnataka), Rasi, Miyams Karchipular (Tamil Nadu), Seva-Automated Milk Collection Centres of Amul dairy cooperatives (Gujarat) and E-Srinkala (Kerala).

Extension is essentially professional activities of educational services which focus on the development of human capital as part of a social system (Veronice, 2015). Agricultural extension is a generic term meaning the application of scientific research and new knowledge to agricultural practices through farmer education. The field of 'extension' now encompasses a wider range of communication and learning activities organized for rural people by educators from different disciplines, including agriculture, agricultural marketing, health and business studies. Agricultural extension program can provide much-needed help in the form of practical field advice, innovations from scientists and practitioners, and sound commodity-marketing principles. Arokoyo (2005) reported that a strong agricultural extension linkage complimented by flawless information flow enhanced by the effective use of information and communication technologies (ICT) would significantly boost agricultural production and improve rural livelihoods in developing countries.

There is a growing recognition that extension must go beyond transferring new food crop technology to farmers and focus on helping the rural poor by promoting agriculture diversification, increasing rural employment helping farmer gain access to biotechnology and access to export markets and also environment awareness and rural health awareness.

Internet is changing all the spheres of human lives. Hence, it is a popular belief that agricultural extension is also no exception to this. It is also expected that the Internet led extension systems are going to act as a key agent for changing agrarian situation and farmers' lives by improving access to information and sharing knowledge. There is an urgent need of internet in agricultural extension, especially in the areas like; to expand knowledge resources, to facilitate better information access, to supplement inadequate technical manpower, for stronger research-extension-client system linkage, to develop efficient feedback mechanism/ for cost-effective extension delivery, to ensure gender equity in technology transfer process, to empower small and marginal farmers, to develop knowledge managers and to serve the farm stakeholders beyond technology transfer role.

The National Commission on Farmers has noted that knowledge deficits constrain agricultural productivity in India. It added that the use of Information and Communication Technologies (ICTs) for agricultural extension is one way of addressing the information needs of farmers. In keeping with this view, the Working Group on Agricultural Extension constituted by the Planning commission (Eleventh Five Year Plan), Government of India, has recommended that there is a need to respond to emerging challenges to the sector by strengthening information dissemination to fanners through the use of ICTs. With the help of ICTs, agricultural extension is expected to become more diversified, Knowledge-intensive, and demand-driven, and thus more effective in meeting farmers' information needs (Fu & Akter, 2012).

Extension personnel are very important in agricultural development process. Specifically the basic role of extension personnel is that it helps in the improvement of those who are involved in primary food production. This is because it involves a shift from the traditional resource-based method of production to a new science-based method. The science-based methods involve the adoption of new varieties, new cultural practices, use of agrochemicals and other capital - intensive inputs. Before these new technologies are adopted, the farmers need to be aware of them and learn how to use them correctly in their farming environment (Pratap, 2016).

Thus, it is the need of the hour to find out the adoption level, usage and perceived benefits of the extension functionaries of Uttarbanga Krishi Vishwavidylaya, Coochbehar (West Bengal) towards IT in general and internet in particular, as a tool of farm advisory services.

2. ROLE OF AGRICULTURAL UNIVERSITIES IN EXTENSION

Agricultural Universities in India are providing extension services to the farmers, agri-business persons and who are engaged in agricultural profession. The universities are providing right type of professionals, in-service training and providing literature and information through ATIC, radio talks, exhibitions, Krishi Melas, Krishi Vichar Manch, etc. The universities are also providing all types of information through training to the farmers in view of plant protection, seed, implements, soils, fruit trees and research on horticulture, marketing, price stabilization, animal husbandry, etc. Now it is necessary to start agro-industries, to reduce the pressure of small land holdings and to generate employment opportunities for community development in collaboration with agricultural universities.

3. RESEARCH PROBLEM

The research problem for the study was "to find out the adoption level, usage and perceived benefits of the extension functionaries of the university towards IT/ICT in general and Internet as a tool of extension in particular".

4. OBJECTIVES OF THE STUDY

In order to respond to the above discussed research questions, the following objectives have been formulated:

- To study the accessibility of Internet services among university extension personnel.
- To study the impact of Internet on farm advisory services.
- To ascertain the constraints perceived in receiving of Internet services.

5. REVIEW OF LITERATURE

Appraisal of previous studies is most useful in any field of investigation. It is integral part of every research endeavor and enables researchers in designing appropriate and in analysing research work. It also provides a basis for the interpretation and representation of findings of the study.

Ganesan *et al.* (2013) conducted a study on "Use of mobile multimedia agricultural advisory systems by Indian farmers: Results of a survey" and showed that majority of the farmers perceived information on pest and disease control as 'most important' and they also felt that accessing information through mobile phone was easy and convenient. Although there were perceived benefits by farmers, the quality of information, timeliness of information and reliability of information were the three important aspects that have to be considered seriously to meet their requirements and prospects in the coming years.

Rizvi (2008) studied the impact of using LifeLines, a mobile-based advisory service for farmers. The study found that there was an increase in the yearly income of the farmers after they received information through LifeLines services.

According to Madukwe (2006), the promise of ICTs in agricultural extension was that they could energize the collection, processing and transmission of data, resulting in faster extension of quality information to more farmers in a bottom- up and interactive channel of communication. Also, increasing the use of ICTs in agricultural extension would narrow the gender disparities in terms of access to agricultural information.

Mruthunjaya and Adhiguru (2005) found that the public

agricultural extension system, which is responsible for disseminating agricultural information to farmers, had become less effective, more time consuming and unsuccessful in meeting the requirements of those involved in agricultural production and there was a gap between the extension agent and the farmers.

Anderson and Feder (2004) revealed in their study that agricultural extension services included transferring knowledge to farmers, advising and educating farmers in their decision making, enabling farmers to clarify their own goals and possibilities, and stimulating desirable agricultural developments. Extension services use a variety of internet-assisted extension programmes to overcome barriers to technological adoption with success.

Annamalai and Rao (2003) conceptualized that private sector initiatives in the area of agricultural extension services delivery were extremely limited. The technologies depended on computers, ICT and land line connections. The problems also included slow and disruptive internet connectivity, poorly maintained land lines, the unreliability of electricity supply and power backup systems and operational constraints from the inadequate maintenance and support of the equipment. They further found that people were benefited by weather information, best agricultural practices, customized crop feedback and quality solutions, intelligent fertilizer and pesticide deployment. Middlemen were eliminated and farmers got better price of their produce.

6. UTTAR BANGA KRISHI VISHWAVIDYALAYA- A BRIEF PROFILE

The northern part of West Bengal is endowed with varied natural resources like forest, economic plant resources, agro-ecosystem etc. and an extremely responsive rural community. Keeping this perspective in view, the state government of West Bengal established a satellite campus of Bidhan Chandra Krishi Viswavidyalaya (BCKV) at Pundibari of Cooch-Behar district in

1979. Later, the State Government strengthened this satellite campus of Bidhan Chandra Krishi Viswavidyalaya further, and ultimately decided to upgrade this campus to a full-fledged State Agricultural University in July 2000 covering the entire North Bengal. The "Uttar Banga Krishi Viswavidyalaya" or UBKV was established by West Bengal Act XX of 2000 and started functioning from 1st February, 2001. The university is comprised of three faculties, viz., faculty of agriculture, faculty of horticulture and faculty of agricultural engineering and 16 departments. The UBKV central library is one of the most important centres of the University, which facilitates the reading, teaching, consultation, study, research and extension programs etc. It also provides different services such as book lending, book bank, reference service, referral service, CD-ROM service, high speed internet facility, Online Public Access Catalogue (OPAC) etc.

Extension education is one of the major functions of the Uttar Banga Krishi Viswavidyalaya. The responsibility for planning, organizing, conducting and coordinating the extension education activities of the university in the northern part of West Bengal lies with the Directorate of Extension Education.

Farm Advisory Service (FAS) is the major wing of the Directorate of Extension Education covering the entire North Bengal through its Krishi Vigyan Kendras (KVKs) located in different districts. Establishment of KVKs accelerated the agricultural production and also improved the socio economic condition of farming community.

Agricultural Technology Information Centre (ATIC) also works under the Directorate of Extension Education. It has been established to provide technical assistance/guidance to the farmers and other related functionaries with the help of Scientists, University Teachers, and Extension Workers.

7. SCOPE OF THE STUDY

The scope of the present study is limited to the extension personnel/specialists/Village Level Workers (VLW) of Uttar Banga

Krishi Viswavidyalaya, Coochbehar, West Bengal.

8. METHODOLOGY

In the present study the universe is very small and specific (Extension personnel of Uttar Banga Krishi Viswavidyalaya, Coochbehar, West Bengal), so for sampling Census method was adopted, i.e. all the extension personnel of the university working at main campus and outstations (all 5 KVKs) were contacted. University extension personnel serving at main campus along with Extension personnel from outstations were taken as the sample. For data collection, a well designed questionnaire was distributed to all the extension personnel (total 76) and 71 had responded timely and positively with the overall response rate being 93.42 per cent.

9. DATA ANALYSIS

An attempt has been made to analyse and interpret the data collected from the respondents of the study. A simple percentage analysis is carried out for the major part of the data analysis to get the relevant results.

Table 1. Age-wise Distribution of the Respondents (n=71)

Age (in years)	Frequency	Percentage
Young (up to 35 years)	17	23.94
Middle Aged (36-50 years)	46	64.79
Old (More than 50 years)	8	11.27
Total	**71**	**100**

Table 1 shows that 64.79 per cent respondents belong to middle-age group, i.e. 36-50 years. The remaining 23.94 per cent respondents belonged to young age group (up to 35 years) and 11.27 per cent respondents belonged to old age group (more than 50 years). Further analysis of data revealed that the majority of the respondents belonged to both the productive age groups which were more enthusiastic as well as mature in extension with deep knowledge and experience.

Table 2. Gender-wise Distribution of the Respondents (n=71)

Age (in years)	Frequency	Percentage
Male	67	94.37
Female	4	5.63
Total	**71**	**100**

Table 2 indicates that majority of the respondents, i.e. 94.37 per cent were male. There were only 5.63 per cent female respondents. The data revealed the male dominance in Extension Advisory Services of the university.

Table 3. Educational status of the Respondents (n=71)

Age (in years)	Frequency	Percentage
B.Sc	52	73.24
M.Sc.	17	23.94
PhD	2	2.82
Post Doctorate	0	0.00
Total	**71**	**100**

Table 3 highlights the educational status of the respondents. It was found that majority of the respondents (73.24 per cent) were Bachelor of Science in Agriculture (B.Sc in Agriculture) and remaining 23.94 percent respondents are Post Graduate (M.Sc.) and only 2.82 percent were Doctorate (PhD). Further analysis of data revealed that majority of the respondents had a deep knowledge of their subject.

Table 4. Length of Service in Extension (n=71)

Length of Service (in years)	Frequency	Percentage
Less than 2	11	15.49
2-5	14	19.71
6-10	24	33.82
11-15	16	22.53
More than 15	6	8.45
Total	**71**	**100**

Table 4 shows that out of total 71 respondents, 33.82 per cent were in extension services for 6-10 years followed by 11-15 years (22.53 per cent), 2-5 years (19.71 per cent), less than 2 years (15.49 per cent) and only 8.45 per cent of the respondents were serving in extension for more than 15 years. Further analysis depicts that the experience of extension personnel/specialists in farm advisory services was very high.

Table 5. Member of Professional Societies (n=71)

Member of Professional Societies	Frequency	Percentage
Not membership of any professional societies	22	30.99
Membership of one society	31	43.66
Membership of two societies	12	16.9
Membership of more than two societies	5	7.04
Office bearer of any societies	1	1.41
Total	**71**	**100**

Table 5 indicates the status of extension personnel of the university as a member of "Professional Society". It clears that 30.99 per cent were 'not member of any professional society. Whereas 43.66 per cent respondents were member of one society. Further analysis of data shows that 7.04 per cent respondents have membership of more than two societies and only 1.41 per cent respondents were office bearer of any society.

Table 6. Type of Training Received (n=71)

Type of Training	Frequency	Percentage
Basic Computer/IT/Internet-based Training	57	80.28
Advance Computer/IT/Internet-based Training	17	23.94
Basic Subject matter Training	65	91.55
Advance Subject matter Training	36	50.7
Basic Extension methods Training	59	83.09
Advance Extension methods Training	28	39.44

*More than one answers were permitted

Table 6 illustrates that 91.55 per cent of the respondents received Basic Subject matter Training. 83.09 per cent respondents underwent basic extension methods training followed by basic IT or computer based training (80.28 per cent), advance subject matter training (50.7 per cent), advance extension methods training (39.44 per cent) and advance IT or computer based training (23.94 per cent).

Table 7. Sources of Information (n=71)

Sources of Information	**Frequency**	**Percentage**
Internet	63	88.73
Television	34	47.89
Radio	13	18.31
Newspaper	15	21.13
Farmers Fairs and Exhibitions	45	63.38
Colleagues	39	54.93
Agricultural Officers' Workshop (AOW)	59	83.09

*More than one answers were permitted

Table 7 reveals the different types of media used by extension personnel and the extent of their utilization for seeking information regarding agriculture. The data pertaining to mass media used by extension personnel presented in the above table clearly indicate that *Internet* ranked first with 88.73 per cent of the respondents. The *Agricultural Officers' Workshop (AOW)* ranked second with 83.09 per cent of the respondents followed by *Farmers Fairs and Exhibitions* ranked third with 63.38 per cent, *Colleagues and peer groups* ranked fourth with 54.93 per cent, and *Television* ranked fifth with 47.89 per cent of the respondents, whereas the respondents had least used the sources like newspapers and radio ranked sixth and seventh respectively with 21.13per cent and 18.31per cent.

Table 8. Internet Usage by the Respondents (n=71)

Internet Usage	Frequency	Percentage
Regularly	43	60.56
Occasionally	16	22.53
Rarely	4	5.63
Never	3	4.23
Can't say	5	7.04
Total	**71**	**100**

Table 8 explains that most half of the respondents (60.56 per cent) used the Internet regularly. While 22.53 per cent used it occasionally followed by 5.63 per cent rarely and 4.23 per cent never used it. 7.04 per cent of the respondents did not choose any option for this question.

Table 9. Internet Usage by the Respondents (n=68)

Skills to Handle and Use Internet Efficiently	Frequency	Percentage
Yes	42	61.76
No	14	20.59
A little bit	12	17.65
Total	**68**	**100**

Table 9 shows 61.76 per cent respondents felt that they had skills to handle and use Internet efficiently. Whereas 20.59 per cent felt that they did not have skills to handle and use Internet efficiently and remaining 17.65 per cent of the respondents felt that they had a little bit of skills to handle and use Internet.

Table 10. Requirement of specialized Training on Internet Usage (n=68)

Training Required	Frequency	Percentage
Yes	52	76.47
No	6	8.82
Uncertain	10	14.71
Total	**68**	**100**

Table 10 illustrates about requirement of specialized training on Internet usage. 76.47 per cent respondents showed their interest in it, 14.71 per cent were uncertain and remaining 8.82 per cent respondents did not show any interest in such training.

Table 11. Purpose of Internet Usage (n=68)

Purpose	Frequency	Percentage
Checking E-Mail	61	89.71
Checking updates in related subject	56	82.35
Reading news	23	33.82
Information about Conferences, Seminars	25	36.76
Official Work	36	52.94
Personal Work	43	63.24
Social Networking	58	85.29
Other reasons	18	26.47

*More than one answers were permitted

Table 11 highlights the various purposes of Internet usage among the respondents. The study found that 89.71 per cent respondents used the Internet for checking E-mail and 85.29 per cent used Internet for social networking. Whereas 82.35 per cent respondents used the Internet for checking updates in related subject followed by 63.24 per cent for personal works, 52.94 per cent for official work, 36.76 per cent for getting information about conferences, seminars, 33.82 per cent for reading news and 26.47 per cent used Internet for other reasons.

Table 12. Purpose of Downloading Information from Internet (n=68)

Purpose of Downloading	Frequency	Percentage
Official	56	82.35
Personal	47	69.12
Capacity building	39	57.35

*More than one answers were permitted

Table 12 describes the purpose of downloading information from Internet. It is revealed that 82.35 per cent of the respondents downloaded the information from the Internet for their official work followed by 69.12 per cent for personal purpose and 57.35 per cent of respondents download information for their capacity building.

Table 13. Contribution of Internet in KVKs (n=68)

Contribution of Internet	Frequency	Percentage
Too much	17	25.00
Much	25	36.76
Adequate	14	20.59
Less	10	14.71
Not at all	2	2.94
Total	**71**	**100**

Table 13 depicts that out of the total respondents, 36.76 per cent were of the view that Internet contributed a lot in efficient functioning of their KVKs. 25 per cent admitted that it contributed significantly/too much, 20.59 per cent admitted that it contributed adequately and 14.71 per cent admitted that it contributed less. Only 2.94 per cent respondents were of the view that Internet did not contribute to the efficient functioning of their KVKs.

Table 14. Impact of Internet on Extension Advisory Services (n=68)

Impact Internet on EAS	Frequency	Percentage
Yes	47	69.12
No	8	11.76
A little bit	13	19.12
Total	**71**	**100**

Table 14 shows that 69.12 per cent respondents accepted contribution of Internet in their activities related to extension advisory services, whereas 19.12 per cent of the respondents considered limited role of Internet in their advisory services. The remaining 11.76 per cent observed that Internet had no role to play in their extension advisory services at all.

Table 15. Benefits of Internet in Farm Advisory Services (n=68)

Benefits of Internet in FAS	**Frequency**	**Percentage**
Full of every type of information	36	52.94
Freedom of thoughts	13	19.12
Convenience communication	43	63.24
Scope to learn something new	59	86.76
Contact with peoples or progressive farmers	17	25.00
Reading e-newspapers, e- magazines, e-journals, e- reports and Govt. e-policies	41	60.29
Efficient broadcasting of government policies	34	50.00
Enhances official efficiency	39	57.35

*More than one answers were permitted

Table 15 revealed the lucrative benefits of Internet in extension/farm advisory services. It is found that scope to learn something new from Internet is responded by 86.76 per cent respondents, followed by convenience communication (63.24 per cent), *reading e-newspapers, e- magazines, e-journals, e- reports and Govt. e-policies* (60.29 per cent), *enhancement of official efficiency* (57.35 per cent) respectively. Similarly, 52.94 per cent respondents find Internet beneficial as it is full of information, while 50 per cent respondents find benefits of Internet in efficient broadcasting of government policies. Apart from it, 25 per cent respondents found Internet as a beneficial tool for *contacting peoples or progressive farmers and* 19.12 per cent found it beneficial as it advocates freedom of thoughts.

Table 16. Effect of Internet on Extension Activities (n=68)

Effect of Internet on Extension	Frequency	Percentage
Cost effective	25	36.76
Speedy reach to various organizations/ progressive farmers for latest information	46	67.65
Contact to large number of farmers at once	35	51.47
Two-way communication	16	23.53
User-friendly	14	20.59
Need of the day	54	79.41

*More than one answers were permitted

Table 16 illustrates the various effects of Internet on extension activities and revealed that majority of respondents, i.e. 79.41 per cent said that Internet is the need of the day, followed by they can quickly reach to various organizations or progressive farmers for latest information (67.65 per cent), contact with large number of farmers at once (51.47 per cent), cost effective (36.76 per cent), Two-way communication (23.53 per cent) and user friendly (20.59 per cent) respectively.

Table 17. Impact of Internet on Personal Adjustment and Well-being (n=68)

Impact of Internet on Personal Adjustment	Frequency	Percentage
Strongly agree	24	35.29
Agree	20	29.42
Neutral	8	11.76
Disagree	12	17.65
Strongly disagree	4	5.88
Total	**71**	**100**

Table 17 highlights the impact of Internet on personal adjustment and well being of the extension personnel. Out of 68 respondents, 35.29 per cent were strongly agreed that over indulgence with Internet affects personal adjustment and well-being, whereas 29.42 per cent respondents were agreed with it.

On the other hand, 17.65 per cent of the respondents were disagreed or strongly disagreed (5.88 per cent). 11.76 per cent respondents stay neutral to this question.

Table 18. Impact of Internet on Moral and Cultural Values (n=68)

Impact of Internet on Moral and Cultural Values	Frequency	Percentage
Strongly agree	18	26.47
Agree	22	32.35
Neutral	12	17.65
Disagree	10	14.71
Strongly disagree	4	5.88
Total	**71**	**100**

Table 18 depicts that out of 68 respondents, most of the respondents were strongly agreed (26.47 per cent) or agreed (32.35 per cent) that use of Internet leaves impact on moral and cultural values. Whereas 14.71 per cent respondents disagreed and 5.88 per cent strongly disagreed. 17.65 per cent respondents were neutral to this statement.

Table 19. Enhancement of Extension Practice through Internet (n=68)

Response	Frequency	Percentage
Strongly agree	26	38.24
Agree	18	26.47
Neutral	13	19.12
Disagree	8	11.76
Strongly disagree	3	4.41
Total	**71**	**100**

Table 19 reveals that out of 68 respondents, most of the respondents were strongly agreed (38.24per cent) or agreed (26.47 per cent) that use of Internet has enhanced their practice of extension. Whereas 11.76 per cent respondents disagreed and

4.41 per cent strongly disagreed. 19.12 per cent respondents were neutral to this statement.

Table 20. Factors limiting the Use of Internet (n=68)

Factors	Frequency	Percentage
Inability of the extension personnel to use Internet	46	67.65
Not enough time to spend on technology	38	55.88
Lack of training	49	72.06
Lack of ICT experience and skills	54	79.41
Lack of technological infrastructure	18	26.47
Cost and lack of funds for equipment	19	27.94
Unsuitable, incompatible, programs	15	22.06

*More than one answers were permitted

Table 20 illustrates that lack of ICT experience and skill was the major constraint among the 79.41 per cent extension personnel, followed by Lack of training (72.06 per cent), inability of the extension personnel to use Internet (67.65 per cent) and not enough time to spend on technology (55.88 per cent). Cost and lack of funds for equipment (27.94 per cent), Lack of technological infrastructure (26.47 per cent) and Unsuitable, incompatible, programs (22.06 per cent) were the other major factors limiting the use of Internet by extension personnel in farm advisory services.

Table 21. Consequences of not Using Internet by Extension Personnel (n=68)

Consequences	Frequency	Percentage
Loss of relevance, confidence and credibility	45	66.18
Loss of contact with timely information	43	63.24
Loss of competitiveness	37	54.41
Isolates extension personnel	39	57.35
Inefficient and inferior service	51	75.00
Loss of production and managementefficiency	34	50.00
Problems in near future	44	64.71

*More than one answers were permitted

Table 21 revealed the consequences of not using Internet as an extension tool by the extension personnel. Inefficient and inferior service was the major consequence (75 per cent), followed by Loss of relevance, confidence and credibility (66.18 per cent), Problems in near future (64.71 per cent), Loss of contact with timely information (63.24 per cent), Isolates extension personnel (57.35 per cent), Loss of competitiveness (54.41 per cent) and Loss of production and management efficiency (50 per cent) respectively.

Table 22. Future Strategies regarding Extension Service (n=68)

Strategies	**Frequency**	**Percentage**
Offline/traditional extension alone	8	11.76
Online/cyber extension alone	13	19.13
Traditional extension as main tool supported by online extension	19	27.94
Online extension as main tool supported by traditional extension	24	35.29
Both having equal role	4	5.88
Total	**71**	**100**

Table 22 describes the future strategies regarding extension advisory services. When the respondents were asked about the strategy to meet out the future challenges of extension advisory services, Online extension as main tool supported by traditional extension was the major strategy of extension advisory services for 35.29 per cent of the respondents followed by Traditional extension as main tool supported by online extension (27.94 per cent), Online/cyber extension alone (19.13 per cent) and Offline/traditional extension alone (11.76 per cent) respectively. Whereas 5.88 per cent responded that offline and online both extension having equal role in extension advisory services.

10. MAJOR FINDINGS OF THE STUDY

- Out of the total extension personnel of UBKV, majority (64.79percent) were middle aged, i.e. 36-50.

- Nearly one-third of the respondents (33.82 per cent) had service in extension for 6-10 years.
- 91.55 per cent of the respondents had gone through basic training on their subject matter.
- Out of this, nearly 50 per cent had basic training and one-third had advanced training.
- The Internet is the most preferred source of information for the extension personnel of the university, followed by Agricultural Officers' Workshop, farmer fairs, friends and relatives, television, newspapers and radio.
- More than half of the respondents (60.56 per cent) used Internet regularly followed by 22.53 per cent occasionally, whereas 5.63 per cent used rarely and 4.23 per cent of the respondents never used Internet.
- The study reveals that more than half of the respondents (61.76 per cent) were capable enough to handle and use Internet properly.
- A majority of the respondents, i.e. 76.47 per cent showed their interest in specialized training on Internet.
- The study illustrates that majority respondents (89.71 per cent) used Internet for checking e-mails, followed by social networking (85.29 per cent), checking updates in allied subject field (82.35 per cent) etc.
- 82.35 per cent of the respondents downloaded the information from the Internet for their official work followed by 69.12 per cent for personal purpose and 57.35 per cent for their capacity building.
- 36.76 per cent respondents were of the view that Internet was of great benefit for efficient functioning of their KVKs/ department.
- The study found that 69.12 per cent respondents accepted the contribution of Internet in the activities related to extension advisory services.

- Scope to learn something new from Internet (86.76 per cent) topped the list as the high benefit of Internet followed by convenience communication (63.24 per cent), reading e-newspapers, e- magazines, e-journals, e- reports and Govt. e-policies (60.29 per cent) etc.
- The study reveals that 79.41 per cent said that Internet is the need of the day, followed by they can quickly reach to various organizations or progressive farmers for latest information (67.65 per cent), contact with large number of farmers at once (51.47 per cent)and cost effective (36.76 per cent) are the other major Internet effects of the extension activities.
- Out of the total respondents, more than one-third (35.29 per cent) were strongly agreed and 29.42 per cent were agreed that over-indulgence with Internet hampered personal adjustments and well-being of extension personnel.
- As far as impact of Internet on moral and cultural values is concerned the most of the respondents were strongly agreed (38.24per cent) or agreed (26.47per cent) and 11.76 per cent were disagreed and 4.41per cent were strongly disagreed.
- As far as the constraints are concerned, the study revealed that lack of ICT experience and skills was the major constraints (79.41 per cent) followed by Lack of training (72.06 per cent), inability of the extension personnel to use Internet (67.65 per cent) and not enough time to spend on technology (55.88 per cent).
- As far as the future strategy concerned, the study revealed that most of the respondents (35.29 per cent) opted for online extension as main tool supported by traditional extension as the major strategy of extension advisory services.

11. RECOMMENDATIONS

The online agricultural extension is a paradigm shift in the mode of the communication and interaction resulting in the qualitative change in the existing practices of agricultural extension. It has not only improved the speed of communication but has also effectively addressed very large audience across large catchments across even in remote parts. Online agricultural extension can be an effective tool of informing the farming community about the government vision, policy and practices within fraction of time. The present study implies that online agricultural extension model can be used as an effective guide for e-governance, information sharing, transparency and addressing public grievance in speedy manner.

12. CONCLUSIONS

Agricultural development can be accelerated and livelihoods can be supported by Internet in so many ways. The dramatic changes that have taken place in the last decade in ICT have touched almost every field of human activity, and agriculture is not an exception. Internet has tremendous potential to revolutionize the way information, knowledge and new technology is managed, developed and delivered to farmers. E-Agriculture can revamp the Extension Advisory Service with providing proper training to extension personnel on ICT and its application in agricultural extension. Internet, the base of ICT, can overcome some of these most challenging issues related to advisory services like accessibility, literacy and language barriers, geographic coverage and local focus.

REFERENCES

Adejo, P. E., & Haruna, U. (2009). Access of farmers to ICTs for agricultural development in Bauchi local government area, Bauchi state. In *Proceedings of the 43rd annual conference of the Agricultural Society of Nigeria*. Abuja.

Anderson, J.R., and Feder, G. (2004). Agricultural extension: Good intentions and hard realities. *World Bank Research Observer, 19*(1), 41–60.

Annamalai, K. and Rao, S. (2003). What Works: ITC's e-choupal and Profitable Rural Transformation, Web-based Information and Procurement tools for Indian Farmers, Retrieved on 24.07.2016 from *http://pdf.wri.org/dd_echoupal.pdf*

Arokoyo, T. (2005). ICTs application in agricultural extension service delivery. In S. Adedoyin (Ed.), *Agricultural Extension in Nigeria* (pp. 245-251). Llorin, Nigeria: Agricultural Extension Society of Nigeria

Duncombe, R and Heeks, R. (2005). Information & Communication Technologies (ICTs), Poverty Reduction and Micro, Small & Medium-scale Enterprises (MSMEs). Retrieved on 24.07.2016 from *https://www.unido.org/fileadmin/media/documents/pdf/Services_Modules/ict_brochure_report.pdf*

Fu, X., & Akter, S. (2012). Impact of mobile telephone on the quality and speed of agricultural extension services delivery: evidence from the rural e-services project in India. In *International Association of Agricultural Economists (IAAE) 2012 Triennial Conference* (pp. 18-24). Foz do Iguaçu, Brazil . Retrieved on July 23, 2016, from *http://www3.qeh.ox.ac.uk/pdf/ptmd/SLPTMD-WP-046.pdf*

Ganesan, M. et al. (2013). Use of mobile multimedia agricultural advisory systems by Indian farmers: Results of a survey. *African Journal of Agricultural Extension and Rural Development, 5*(4), 89-99.

Lokanathan, S., De Silva, H. and Fernando, I. (2011). Price transparency in agricultural produce markets: Sri Lanka. In D. J. Grimshaw & S. Kala (Eds.), *Strengthening Rural Livelihoods. The impact of information and communication technologies in Asia* (pp. 15-32). Practical Action Publishing.

Madukwe, M.C. (2006). Delivery of Agricultural Extension Services to Farmers in Developing Countries. Retrieved on 26.07.2016 from *http://knowledge.cta.int/Dossiers/S-T-Policy/Participatory-approaches-in-ARD/Feature-articles/Delivery-of-Agricultural-Extension-Services-to-Farmers-in-Developing-Countries*

Mruthunjaya and Adhiguru, A. (2005). ICT for Livelihood Security: A Reality Check. *Mainstreaming ICTs, 2*(2), 14-18.

Pratap, B. (2016). Impact of Internet on Extension Specialists for Farm Advisory Services: A case study of CCS Haryana Agricultural University, Hisar. In Pratap et al. (Ed.), *Transformation of Library Services in Electronic Era* (pp. 55-80). New Delhi: Studera Press.

Raabe, K. (2008). Reforming the Agricultural Extension System in India: What we know about what works where and why? : International Food Policy Institute. Retrieved on 26.07.2016 from *https://core.ac.uk/download/files/153/6388476.pdf*

Rizvi, S.M.H. (2008). LifeLines: livelihood solutions through mobile technology in India. In D. J. Grimshaw & S. Kala (Eds.), *Strengthening Rural Livelihoods. The impact of information and communication technologies in Asia* (pp. 53-70). Practical Action Publishing.

Veronice. (2015). Analysis Level of Utilization Information and Communication Technology with: The Competency Level of Extension Workers. *International Journal on Advanced Science, Engineering, 5*(3), 226-229.

7

Library Usage Patteren Among Teaching and Non Teaching Staff of Nehru College, Pailapool, Cachar (Assam)

Sangita Yadav
Research Scholar, Department of Library and Information Science, Assam University, Silchar

ABSTARCT

A library is fundamentally an organized set of resources, which include human services as well as the entire spectrum of media (e.g., text, video, hypermedia). Libraries have physical components such as space, equipment, and storage media; intellectual components such as collection policies that determine what materials will be included and organizational schemes that determine how the collection is accessed; and people who manage the physical and intellectual components and interact with users to solve information problems.

Library is important not only for students but also for teachers. College library performs an important function in the educational process. The Teaching and Non Teaching Staff of the colleges are using library for different purposes. As we know that many resources are available to the libraries of the college. In view of knowing the extent of library usage pattern of Teaching and Non Teaching Staffs, this study has been carried out and many important findings are emerged which have opened new areas of further research in the area of library usage pattern.

For the present study survey method was adopted using Questionnaire and Interview schedule as tools of data collection. On the basis of responses received, data was tabulated and analysed using SPSS and Ms-Excel. The important survey findings in respect of demographic profiles of students and their library usage Pattern among Teaching and Non Teaching Staffs, of Nehru College.

1. INTRODUCTION

Education is a process of learning, with the aim to develop the capabilities in the people at all levels. In this process schools, colleges and universities play a vital role. The present educational system in India comprises both academic and professional studies by offering courses leading to bachelor's and master's degrees. This system has evolved over the last 150 years. It was initiated by the British rulers of the country and after 4947 it was developed by independent India with appropriate changes and modifications. In the last fifty years, the educational system has been reviewed by high powered commissions set up by the Government of India at different times, in order to introduce appropriate measures to improve the quality of education and make it more relevant to the country's requirements. In recent years, the government has been very much concerned with educational reforms, especially at the school level. The nation adopted a new educational policy in 1986 in order to provide the best education to our children, wherein we are in tune with our national heritage as well as modern with advances in science, technology and management (IGNOU, 2010).

In all these efforts to modernize our educational system, libraries and self-learning have been considered vital components and integral parts of the entire educational process. Considerable thought and attention have been given to the planning and development of academic libraries and self-learning at all levels. As principal instruments of the modern educational system; there is, however, still scope for improvement in terms of their effectiveness.(IGNOU 2010)

1.1. Background of the Study

A library plays a very vital role throughout the life. Particularly College library is very important not only for students and but also for Teachers. Some of the books are very rare which are not available in the market but they can be availed from libraries. Some books like dictionary, Encyclopaedia and other subjects are very costly.One can get such type of books issued from libraries.A good and efficient library will certainly help students as well as the Teachers in many ways to meet the new challenges they start facing at college. The main aim of this study is in order to ascertain how Teaching andNon Teaching Staffs of Nehru College use the Library.

1.2. Objectives of the study

The objectives of the study are:

1. To study the Status of Library Usage Pattern among Teaching and Non-Teaching Staffs of Nehru college ;
2. To Study the Purpose for visit Library ;
3. To Study the Frequency of Library visit Teaching and Non-Teaching Staffs of Nehru college ;
4. To Study the Difficulties faced by the Teaching and Non-Teaching Staffs in accessing Library information/Resources;

1.3. Scope of the Study

Library plays a very Important role not only on Students but also in Teahers life. Libraries provide the teachers very healthy environment. In a library, atmosphere is very calm and disciplined. It helps students and Teachers to keep very good concentration on their studies and also preparing their Notes. Libraries are the only place where we are free from all conventions because reading is absolutely a matter of personal Choice.The present study has been undertaken with a view to know the Usage of Library among the Teaching and Non-Teaching Staffs of Nehru college, Pailapool, Cachar (Assam).

1.4. Limitation of the Study

- The study has been further delimited to the Teaching and Non-Teaching Staffs of Nehru college only ;
- The data pertaining to the study were collected through the Questionnaires, Interview-Schedule and Personal Observation.
- The reliability of the facts depends on the honesty of the respondents.

2. REVIEW OF LITERATURE

For the present study the primary as well as the secondary source of literatures has been consulted. Some journal articles and theses have also been consulted. Previously many studies have been carried out in recent years on use of Internet in university library (Mishra and Satyanarayana, 2001) Internet for Libraries. (Kamlavijayan, 2001); Internet and its use in SJCE (Kumbar and Shirun, 2003); Internet usage by students and faculty members of Kuvempu University (Birader, Rajashekhar, and Sampat Kumar, 2004); Use of Internet by teachers and students in ShaheedBhagat Singh College of Engineering and Technology (Rajiv Kumar and Amritpal Kaur 2004); Internet use by the researchers in Punjab University, Chandigarh (Mahajan 2005); Internet use by the Research Scholars in University of Delhi (Madhusudan, 2007); Use of Internet in Engineering College of thee Districts of Karnataka State (Kumbhar and Vasunatha 2007); Sharma, Singh and Mishra, 2008 has also studied the usage pattern of Internet by the teachers and research scholars of Kurushetra University; Use of Internet by the Students of Bidhan

Chandra KrishiViswavidyalaya (West Bengal) (Das and Basu (2009); and Use of Internet among the Research Scholars of the Faculty of Science, University of Allahabad (Devender Kumar and Shukla, 2009).

Status of Internet and Social Media Usage Pattern among the Media Professionals of North East India (Sinha, M. K., Bhattacharjee, S., &Bhattacharjee, S. 2014); Status of Internet and Social Media Usage Pattern among Media Professional of Cachar and Guwahati (Sinha, M.K and Yadav, S 2017), There are many studies conducted on the Internet and Social Media usage pattern, no comprehensive and substantial studies have been carried out on usage of Library. Therefore, in present studies an attempt has been taken to study the Library usage Pattern among Teaching and Non Teaching Staffs of Nehru College.

3. RESEARCH METHODOLOGY AND RESEARCH DESIGN

3.1. Source of Data

In the present study, the Survey method of research has been adopted using structured Questionnaire as a tool for collection of data. The questionnaire was designed keeping in view of the stated objectives and the structured questionnaire comprises mainly of closed ended-questions.

3.2. Tools for Data Collection

The tools of data collection translate the research objectives into specific questions/item, the response to which will provide the data required to achieve the research objectives. The following tools were used for collection of data pertaining to the present study.

3.2.1. Questionnaire

Questionnaire is widely used tool for data collection in research. It is a systematic compilation of questions logically related to problem under study. It has been assured that the information given by them would be used for the research purpose only would be kept be confidential.

3.2.2. Personal Interview

The researcher also adopt personal interview for the collection of more reliable data. Personal interview were arranged with the Teaching and Non-Teaching Staffs of Nehru college giving prior intimation to the respondents. The interviews were conducted according to an interview schedule.

3.2.3. Description of Questionnaire

The designed questionnaire consists of two main parts. First part consists of *"Personal details"*, second part consists of *"Library usage pattern among Teaching and Non-Teaching Staffs of Nehru college"*.

3.3. Data Analysis

On the basis of collected data the questionnaire/interview data is coded tabulated analysed to come on the findings and conclusion. All the results have been presented in the form of tables and/or graphs. SPSS/MS-Excel (Software's) was used for data analysis and interpretation.

4. ANALYSIS OF DATA AMONG TEACHING AND NON TEACHING STAFFS OF NEHRU COLLEGE, PAILAPOOL, CACHAR(ASSAM)

A. Personal Background of the Respondents / Demographic Characteristics of the Respondents Personal Information of Teaching and Non Teaching Staffs

4.1. Distribution of Questionnaire to Respondent and Responses Received

To know the response rate altogether 28 questionnaire were distributed among the Teaching and Non Teaching Staffs of Nehru College out of which, 24 (85.71%) respondents have responded. Thus the response rate is 85.71%.

Table 1. Responses Received from the Respondents (N=28)

Questionnaire	Nos.	Percentage (%)
Received	24	85.71
Not received	4	14.28
Total	**28**	**100.00**

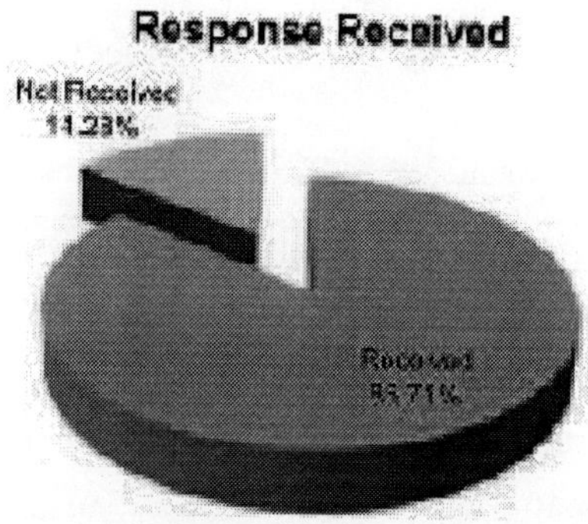

Fig. 1. Responses Received from the Respondents

4.2. Gender Wise Distribution of Respondents

The Survey result as shown in Table -2 shows gender –wise distribution of respondents which indicates that number of male respondents 19 (79.16%) is more than that of female respondents 5 (20.83%), although equal number of questionnaire were distributed amongst the male and female students. While making comparison between male and female respondents, it reveals that the percentage of male respondents is high in comparison to female respondents.

Table 2. Gender Wise Distribution of Respondents (N=24)

Sex	No of Respondents	Percentage (%)
Male	19	79.16
Female	5	20.83
Total	**24**	**100**

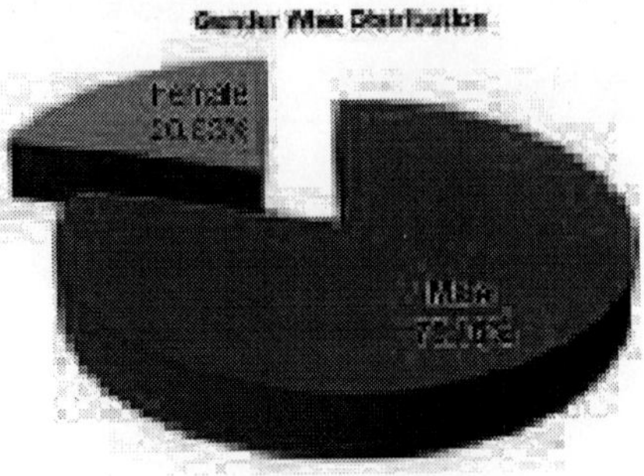

Fig. 2. Gender Wise Distribution of Respondents

4.3. Purpose of Library Visit of Students

To know the purpose of library visit of Students, questionnaire send to respondents and the result reveals that 15(2.5%) respondent's visits library for reading books newspaper etc. Whereas 10(41.66%) respondents visit for internet searching where only 5(20.83%) respondents visits for other purpose in the library.

Table 3. Purpose of Library Visit

Purpose of Library Visit	No of Respondents	Percentage (%)
For Reading books, newspaper etc.	15	62.5
For Internet Search	10	41.66
Other Purpose	5	20.83

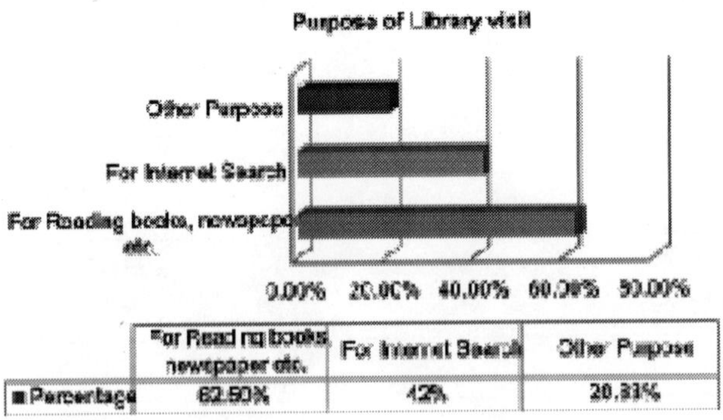

Fig. 3. Purpose of Library Visit

4.4. Frequency of Library Visit of Students

The survey results as shown in table no -4 reveals the frequency of library visits of the respondents which shows that out of 24 respondents, most of the respondents (29.16%) visits library on daily basis which is followed by 6 (25%) respondents who visit library on weekly basis whereas 5 (20.83%) respondents visit on fortnightly basis, 4(16.66%) Monthly basis and only 2(8.33%) respondents are not regular who visit library.

Table 4. Frequency of Library Visit of user (N=24)

Frequency	No of Respondents	Percentage (%)
Daily	7	29.16
Weekly	6	25
Fortnightly	5	20.83
Monthly	4	16.66
Not Regular	2	8.33
Total	**24**	**100**

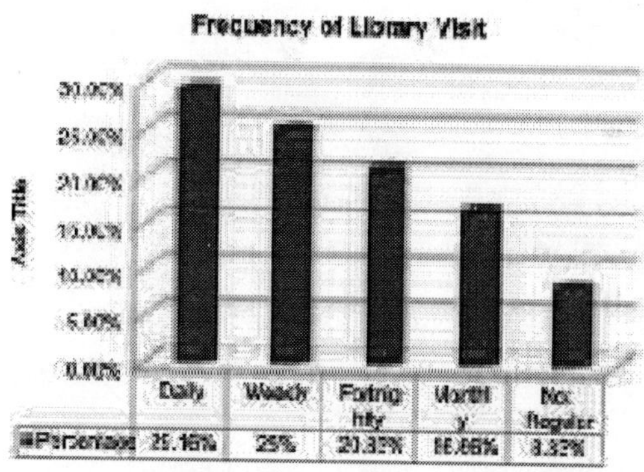

Fig. 4. Frequency of Library Visit of user

4.5. Difficulties faced by users in accessing to library information

The survey findings as shown in Table 6 which reveals that out of 24 respondents 8(33.33%) students facing problem because of non-availability of adequate reading material which is followed by 7(29.16%) and also7(29.16%) because of because of lack of time whereas only 2(8.33%) facing problem lack of Awareness of Internet.

Table 5. Difficulties faced by users in accessing library information (N=24)

Types of problem	No of Respondents	Percentage (%)
Non availability of adequate reading material	8	33.33
Lake of awareness of Internet	2	8.33
Lake of time to visit library	7	29.16
Other Problem	7	29.16
Total	**24**	**100.00**

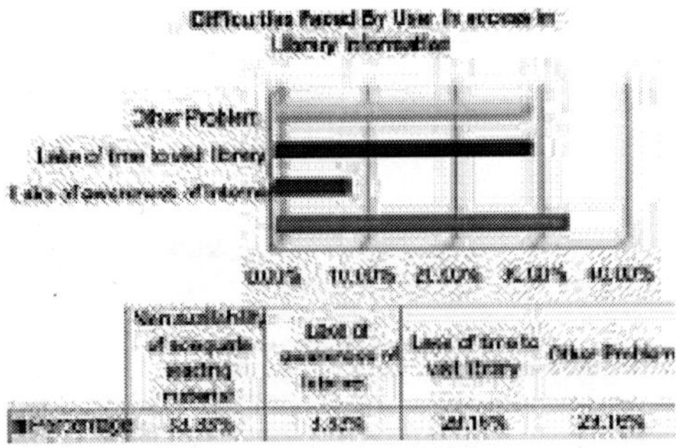

Fig. 5. Difficulties faced by users in accessing library information

5. SUGGESTIONS AND RECOMMENDATION'S

1. College Library should organize User Awareness Programme and Computer/ Internet Awareness Programme for the students as well as for teaching and Non Teaching Staffs for optimum utilization of on-line resources;
2. More computers/ terminals with latest configurations should be made available in the library to access Internet in general;
3. To maintain their interest towards optimum usage of e-resources amongst the students;

4. The library should ensure uninterrupted power supply for better use of Library Services;
5. The Libraries of need to develop adequate collection and development policy for acquiring reading material need to be changed.

6. CONCLUSION

A library plays a very vital role throughout the life. Particularly College library is very important not only for students and but also for Teachers. Some of the books are very rare which are not available in the market but they can be availed from libraries. Some books like dictionary, Encyclopaedia and other subjects are very costly.One can get such type of books issued from libraries.A good and efficient library will certainly help students as well as the Teachers in many ways to meet the new challenges they start facing at college.

The study shows that Library plays a very important role in Staffs who are working in the colleges bacause they also takes help from the resources which are available in the library. As we know that many e-resources are available in the internet as open source resources, the Staffs also get benefited from those resources which are available in library.

The present study is based on the survey of Library Usage Pattern among Teaching and Non Teaching Staffs of Nehru College. The survey findings are interesting.The paper also highlights the important survey findings in respect of demographic profile of Teaching and Non Teaching Staffs and also highlighting their Library use pattern.The paper also highlighted some problems in accessing to information and put forward some suggestion for the overall improvements of Library services.

REFFERENCES

1. Biradar, B.S., Rajashekhar, G.R. and Kumar, S.(2004). A Study of Internet Usage by Students and faculties in Kuvempu University. *Library Herald*, 44 (4),: 283-294.

2. Das, A. and Basu. D. (2009). Use of Internet by the Students of Bidhan Chandra KrishiViswavidyalaya (West Bengal): A Survey . In: Library/ Information Users in Digital Era (*Eds*: Amitabha Chatterjee *et al.*,)*.XXVII All India IASLIC Conference/ 26-29 December, 2009/ KIIT Bhubaneswar/ NO.48/* pp39-47.

3. Kumar, D and Shukla, S.K. (2009). Use of Internet among the Research Scholars of the Faculty of Science, University of Allahabad: A Case Study . In: Library/ Information Users in Digital Era (*Eds*: Amitabha Chatterjee et al.,)*.XXVII All India IASLIC Conference/ 26-29 December, 2009/ KIIT Bhubaneswar/ NO.48/*pp 246-253

4. Kumar, D and Shukla, Kumar, S. (2009). Use of Internet among the Research Scholars of the Faculty of Science, University of Allahabad: A Case Study . In: Library/ Information Users in Digital Era (*Eds*: Amitabha Chatterjee et al., *).XXVII All India IASLIC Conference/ 26-29 December, 2009/ KIIT Bhubaneswar/ NO.48/*pp 246-253.

5. Kamlavijayan , D. (2001). Internet for Libraries. *Kelpro Bulletin,* 5 (1), 45-48.

6. Kumbar, M. and Shirun, S.(2003). Internet and its use in SJCE : A Case Study. *SRELS :Journal of Information Management* , 40 (2), 160-176.

7. Kumbhar, M., &Vasunatha, R. (2007). Use of Internet in Engineering College of thee Districts of Karnataka States : A Study. *ILA Bulletin, 43*(1), 13-18.

8. Kumbhar, M., &Vasunatha, R. (2007). Use of Internet in Engineering College of thee Districts of Karnataka States : A Study. *ILA Bulletin, 43*(1), 13-18.

9. Madhusudan, M. (2007). Internet Use by Research Scholars in University of Delhi. *Library Hi-Tech News, Emerald Group Publishing Limited, 24*(8), 6-42.

10. Mahajan P.(2005). Internet Use by Researcher: A Study of Punjab University, Chandigarh. *Library Practice & Philosophy*, 8 (2).

11. Sinha, M. K., Bhattacharjee, S., &Bhattacharjee, S. (2014). Status of Internet and Social Media Usage Pattern among the Media Professionals of North East India. *International Journal of Modern Electronics and Communication Engineering (IJMECE, 2*(3). Retrieved from http://ssrn.com/abstract=2585051,(Retrieved on 09.04.2015, at 22.26).

12. Sinha, M.K. (2009). A Study on ICT and Internet Awareness amongst the Research Scholars and University Teachers: A Case Study. *INFOLIB,* 2 (1-4), 2009.

13. Sinha, M.K.(2010). Internet Awareness and Internet Usage Pattern amongst University and College Teachers of North Eastern Region of

India: A Survey. *Library Progress (International)*, 30 (1), 2010, 61-82 (ISSN : 0970-1052).

14. Importance of Library in the Student Life - Boddunan. (n.d.). Retrieved from https://www.boddunan.com/articles/miscellaneous/51-general-reference/12436-importance-of-library-in-the-student-life.html.
15. Untitled Document. (n.d.). Retrieved from https://ils.unc.edu/~march/cacm95/mainbody.htm.

8

Web-Based Services in Libraries

Vijay Kumar Bharati
Senior Assistant Librarian, Central Library,
Mahatma Gandhi Kashi Vidyapith, Varanasi (UP)

Learning and education are important dimension in the growth of human society. The Internet has come up as a medium to import education and supplement the traditional teaching multimedia learning objects include text, audio, video and graphics as a carry medium for offered contents. The library services should be designed keeping in mind the current generation of users. Web – based services are increasingly being used in libraries with the development in technology and change in the user's requirements. Web2.0 technologies have made it possible to customize libraries websites and introduce space for interaction with theirs users. Libraries are introducing web 2.0 features in their website and in cooperating blogs and wikis. Web –based application are simple and easy to use and can be used for designing useful library services without financial expenditure. The web2.0 applications enable the libraries to be socially interlinked with other applications and communities. Web-Based Library Services are mainly provided through the library portal which is a special kind of gateway to web based libraries using this media to publicize their contents so that the users can take advantage of all the lectures and important meeting which they might have missed. Libraries are uploading content on You Tube that is useful to maximum number of people.

Twitter

Twitter is also quite popular these days. The messages by the people for the people in the form of tweets help to know about the views of a particular person over an issue. The reaction on a tweet by the other people by following the same tweet shows that they are really interested in the discussion. In libraries, Librarians are also using Twitter to get users reactions over some important issues. As this is a real time work and instant responses one can get, shows the popularity of Twitter in the libraries. Libraries like Delhi Public Library, Library of congress and Indian Prairies Libraries use Twitter to make their patrons and the professionals to stay connected all the time. Information regarding latest advancements can be shared by library professions to the patrons and also can get their opinions regarding the same issue.

Twitter service at Delhi Public library

Wikis

Wikis are collaborative web pages allowing for high user

participation. They allow users to create web pages and documents as a collaborative community. Wiki users can edit the content as they read and related pages are linked with in the text to make it easy to move from the wiki to another related site. Within academic libraries, Wikis are primarily used for the creation of collaborative subject guides. Academic libraries can create subject Wikis with links to resources on a chosen topic or for a particular class, including information regarding relevant databases and search tips tailored to that subject.

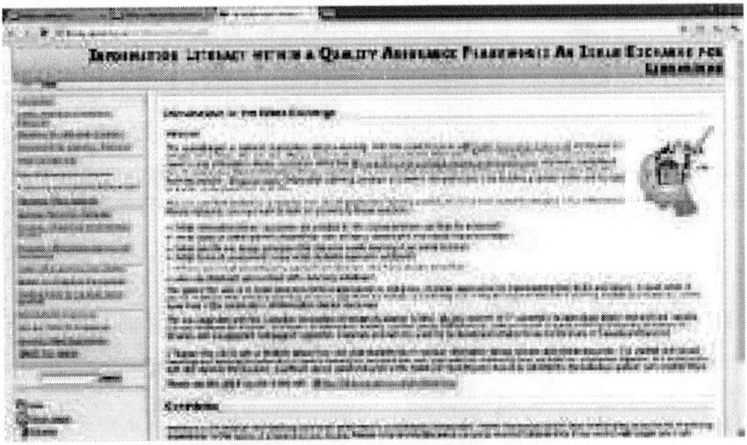

Wiki service at Queen's University Library

Web OPAC

Web OPAC is a library catalog on the web. Users can search the required information by connecting to Uniform Resource Locator (URL) of Web OPAC at anytime from anywhere in the world. It facilitates the users to access the bibliographic details of holdings in the collection of particular library. In this system the library books and other reading items are arranged according to the subject content that is given a call number. Some of the major services available through Web OPAC are library catalogue, search facility on entire database, group wise restricted access for users and guest.

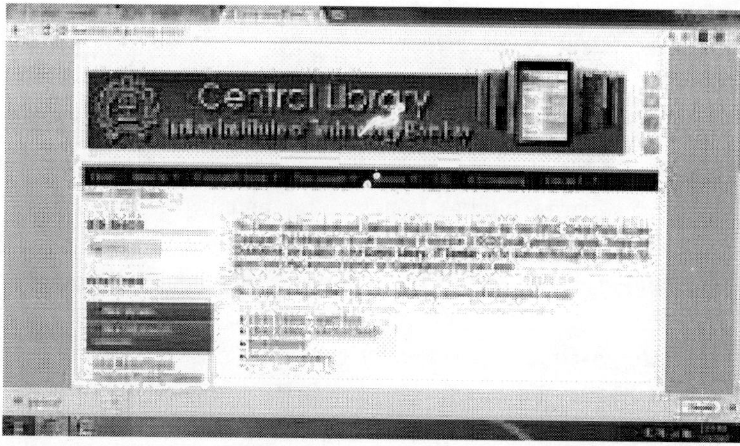

Web OPAC in Central Library IIT Bombay

LibraryThing

According to Wikipedia LibraryThing is a social cataloguing web application for storing and sharing book catalogs and various types of book metadata. The primary feature of LibraryThing is the cataloguing of books by importing data from libraries through Z39.50 connections.

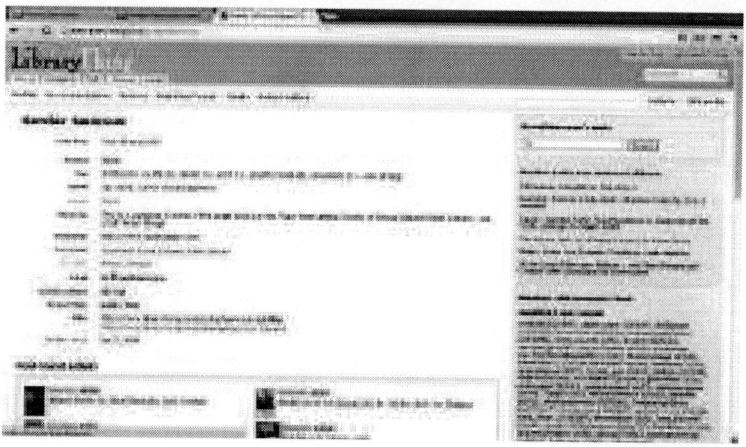

LibraryThing service at Country of Prince Edward Public Library

Blogs

Blog is an online diary where one can post information (not only text but also audio, photographs and videos) on a regular basis. There are some related terms in creating blogs like blogger, blogging, blogging software, blogrolling, blogsphere. Blogging software makes it easier for people to create blogs. Blogrolling is the act of moving from one blog to another and blogosphere is the world or community of blogs and blogging. Libraries are quite aware to use blogs in their routine as lots of blogs are written every day by the librarians to inform their patrons about the latest advance in the field of Library and Information Science. It helps the people to know about others view on certain issues by commenting on a particular blog. Library users also eagerly wait to update themselves by reading useful blogs.

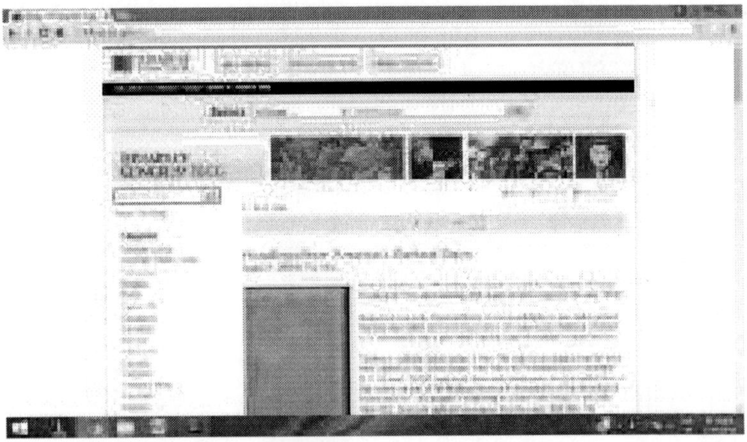

Blogs service at Library of Congress

Podcasting

It is a type of digital media consisting of an episode series of audio files subscribed to and download through web syndication or streamed online to a computer or mobile device. British Library is using this tool to audio sounds to disseminate to its users.

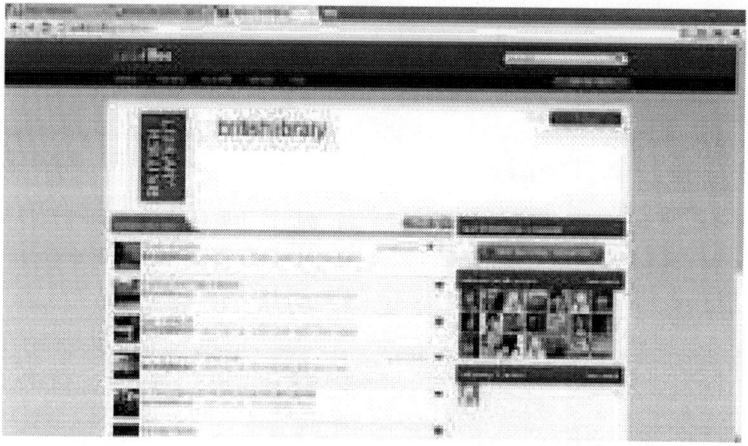

Podcasting service at British Library

Flickr

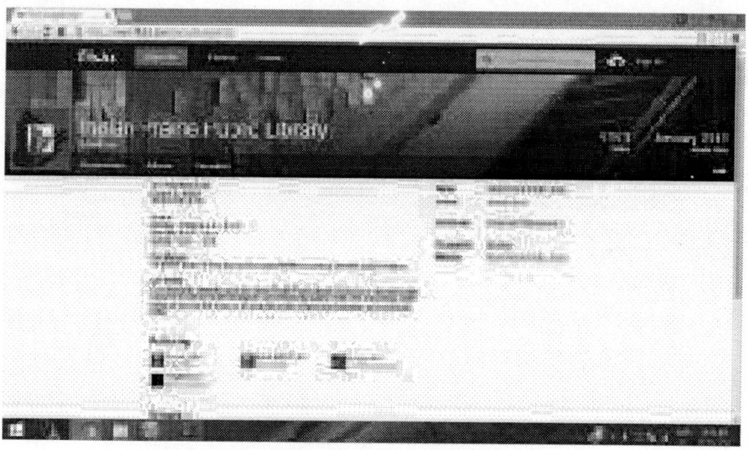

Flickr's service at Indian Pairie Library

Flickr is used to share pictures and photographs. It is one of the famous tools in web service. The two main uses of Flickr are for recording events and promoting collections of Libraries. Other specified uses included tours of libraries, providing photos to press and social media for promotional purposes, photography competitions, sharing information about library initiatives with other library professionals, exhibits at shows, advertising the library building, display of heritage images and fun. Recording events, promoting collections and services dominate the public library use of Flickr. What is available, both collection and services and the recording of events (as both a promotion and a record) can be shared. Flickr allows an easy sharing of images of events and people can comment on the library images including events in which they participated.

Digg

Digg is a social news website. Its originalities lies in such library operations where the users are allowed to vote for web content up or down that is called digging. The Digg service in Indira Gandhi National Open University's library is used to submit content from the user's side.

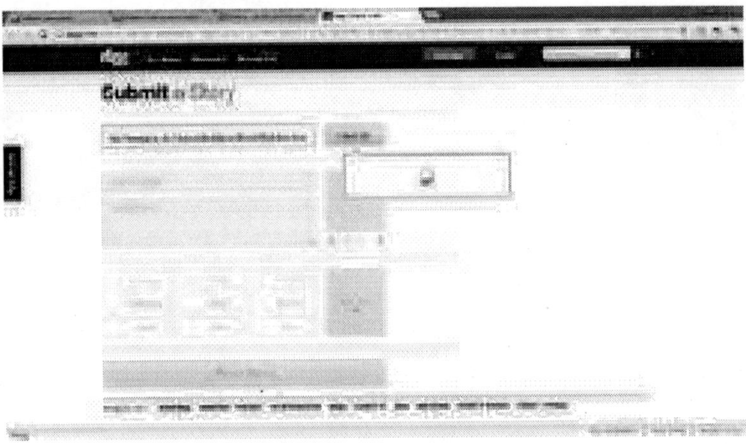

Digg service at IGNOU's Library

Slide Share

According to Wikipedia, Slide share is a web2.0 based slide hosting service. Library professionals can upload files privately or publicly for the use of the patrons so that the users of libraries may be demonstrated some of the important topics through the library's website.

Slide Share service at Ohio Public Library

LIBRARIES AND WEB –BASED SERVICES IN PRESENT SCENARIO

- Libraries are using You Tube videos as a marketing channel and also an educational medium.
- Many Libraries are using web-based tools to educate users and marketing of resources and services.
- Many libraries will seek ways to create mobile apps for providing various services and not just from its website.
- As more database vendors create mobile apps, libraries will be able to offer more services to patrons via mobile.
- Book review sites such as Good reads and Library thing will be used by more libraries as tool for offering book reviews and for locating new books to read.
- Libraries can use online gaming sites as a marketing tool.
- Libraries can use Google apps for a variety of functions including e-mail.

CONCLUSION

The popularity of Internet and web-based services in libraries have influenced the behaviours of the users. Lib2.0 is the applications of users oriented, interactive, collaborative and multimedia library services. A number of web-based service and social media such as face book, disc, like den blogs wikis have provided a platform to theirs users where they can share collaborate and publish their data, wikis and blogs can be used by the libraries for manually of library services on the web. The social networking websites can be used for communicating with users spread over wider area. Webpage can be used for providing information about latest book resources and services. Social book marking websites can be used to facilitate users to create and share book marks. Blogs can be used for receiving feed books from users about library services and resources and also used for interaction with users, facilities web- based services can be used for creating awareness about the services and resources being provided by library. Common examples of Web-based services are the popular social networking sites like Face book, MySpace, YouTube, Flickr, etc. With the help of web-based services, libraries can promote their users, services, resources, events and communication. Study concludes that according to the changing needs of library users, libraries need to be changed accordingly. Libraries should be facilitated with internet service and develop their web page and social media page. Finally we can say that web technology has given powers to library users towards controlling their subscription and expressly their needs. Further the web technology has improved the library users to be more interactive with the existing library services which are available on the web.

REFERENCES

1. Bhatnagar, Anjana. (2005). Web Based Library Services.3rd convention PLANNER-2005, Assam University, Silchar, Ahmedabad.
2. Hatua, SR. Seminar on web based library and information services, DRTC. (http://shatua.tripod.com/DRTCseminar.html)
3. Jeyshankar, R. and Babu, Ramesh B. (2009). Websites of universities in Tamil Nadu: a webometric study. Annals of Library and Information Studies, 56, 69-79.

4. Madhusudhan, M., & Nagabushnam, V. (2012). Use of web based library services in select university libraries in India: A study. International Journal of Library and Information Studies, 2 (1). Retrieved from http://ijlis.org/img/2012_2_issue_1/1_20.pdf.

5. Pathak, S.K., Mishra, A., and Sahoo, G. (2008). Future of web based library and information services: An Indian scenario. 6th convention PLANNER-2008, Nagaland University. Retrieved from http://ir.inflibnet.ac.in/handle/1944/1156

6. Arora, Jagdish. (2001). Web Based Digital Resources and Services: Trends and Innovations. CALIBER- 2001. Pune. http://hdl.handle.net/1944/105

7. Sangale,D.B. (2015). ICT application and web based services in Library and Information Science. ASM's International E-Journal on ongoing research in Management and IT, 9-14.

8. Walsh Bill. Mass Media and Cultural Literacy.Retrieved (visited on 15 May, 2018). *http://jcp.proscenia.net/publications/articles_mlr/walsh/massmedia.html.*

9. http://en.wikipedia.org/wiki/social_media (visited on 15 May, 2018).

10. http://youtube.com/delhipublibrary/ (visited on 15 May, 2018).

11. http://www.youtube.com/libraryofcongress/ (visited on 15 May, 2018).

12. http://www.facebook.com/libraryofcongress/ (visited on 15 May, 2018).

13. http://www.facebook.com/pages/Delhi-Public-Library/149880051689736/ (visited on 15 May, 2018).

14. http://blogs.loc.gov (visited on 15 May, 2018).

15. http://www.flickr.com/libray of congress/ (visited on 15 May, 2018).

16. http://www.flickr.com/photos/delhipubliclibrary (visited on 15 May, 2018).

17. http://twitter.com/delhipublibrary (visited on 15 May, 2018).

18. http://twitter.com/librarycongress/ (visited on 15 May, 2018).

19. http://library.queensu.ca/wiki/elearning/doku.php/ (visited on 15 May, 2018).

20. http://en.wikipedia.org/wiki/SlideShare/ (visited on 15 May, 2018).

21. http://www.slideshare.net/OPLIN/ (visited on 15 May, 2018).

22. http://www.librarything.com/profile/teenroom, (visited on 15 May, 2018).

23. http://digg.com/submit?partner=addthis&url=http%3A%2F%2Fwww.ignou.ac.in (visited on 15 May, 2018).

9

Web Based Resources: Institutional Repositories

Vijay Prakash Singh
Asstt. Librarian, Dr. Bhagwandas Central Librarym
M.G.K.V. Varanasi

A web resource is a unit of information on the World Wide Web that has an identity and is identified by Uniform Resource Identifiers (URI). Web resources are accessed and browsed using HTTP protocol and files are exchanged using FTP. Web resources are networked, re-aggregated, heterogeneous and available in multimedia formats. There is a vast array of digital data formats: text, hypertext, image, sound, video, animation, etc." Web-based resources are collections of links to other sites or combinations of links each resource is described by one or more concepts and is identified by its URL, and can be accessed by one or more keywords describing its content

According to **Lavoie and Nielsen** (1999) **Web Resource** is a resource, identified by a URI (Uniform resource identifier), that is a member of the Web core. Web core is "The collection of resources residing on the Internet that can be accessed using any implemented version of HTTP as part of the protocol stack (or its equivalent), either directly or via an intermediary".

A web resource can be defined as: "A productive resource

that is stationed on the World Wide Web and has an identity and the identity in case of web resource is Uniform Resource Identifier (URI)". World Wide Web is a vast source of information that hosts a number of web resources. Examples of web resources include e-journals, e-books, online databases, e-theses/dissertations, subject gateway portals, web OPAC, institutional repositories, blogs, e-lectures etc.

INSTITUTIONAL REPOSITORIES

Institutional repositories (IR) are a new breed of services and software, still in their nascence. The technology is constantly changing and new information on building and running these services is published all the time. An institutional repository is not defined solely by the software and database that contain digital collections. It is a set of services for those who deposit content, the academic and research communities. Institutional Repository is an online archive of scholarly output of faculty members, research scholars and other community members of the institution. An Institutional Repository collects preserves and disseminates the intellectual output of an institution. IR may include in its collection a wide variety of documents such as research articles and scholarly papers, conference proceedings, working papers or technical reports, computer programs, data sets, electronic theses and dissertations. IR can be created and developed using any one of a number of software available for building them. Examples of prominent Institutional Repository are DSpace, EPrints, Fedora and Bepress. Institutional repository is a valuable asset to its institution it helps creating global visibility for an institution's scholarly output, improved visibility of the research output hence results in greater citations of the research publications of the institutions as the content of the repository can be searched and accessed globally, it serves as an archive for the digital preservation of the valuable research output of the institution.

DEFINITION

An Institutional Repository has been defined by Lynch (2003) as "a university based Institutional Repository is a set of services that a university offers to the members of its community for the management and dissemination of digital materials created by the institution and its community members". It is most essentially an organizational commitment to the stewardship of these digital materials, including long-term preservation where appropriate, as well as organization and access or distribution."

An another important definition of Institutional Repository was put forward by Crow (2002) which is "a digital archive of the intellectual product created by the faculty, research staff, and students of an institution and accessible to end users both within and outside of the institution, with few if any barriers to access".

The SPARC organization provided More comprehensive definition of institutional repositories as:

- Institutionally defined
- Scholarly
- Cumulative and perpetual
- Open and interoperable

Hence an institutional repository is a set of services that an institute/university offers to the members of its community for the management and dissemination of digital materials created by the institution and its community members. An effective institutional repository necessarily requires collaboration among librarian, information technologists, archives and record managers faculty and administration and policy makers.

ELEMENTS OF AN INSTITUTIONAL REPOSITORY SYSTEM

Crow (2002) proposed some essential elements of an institutional repository as follows:

Institutionally defined : Institutional repositories contain the scholarly and research output of an institution and specifically aims to preserve the entire intellectual output of the institution.

Scholarly Content : An institutional repository may contain any scholarly content created by researchers of the institution. Scholarly content of the institutional repository may include research articles, conference papers, electronic theses and dissertations, and gray literature.

Cumulative and perpetual : The content or the materials once submitted in an Institutional Repository should not be withdrawn except in rare cases such as of plagiarism or copyright infringement. Institutional repository systems must be able to accommodate and preserve a large number of documents that are submitted every year to on a long-term basis.

Open and interoperable : Institutional Repository should be open access so that it provides easy and barrier free access to the intellectual output generated by the institution and thus increasing awareness about the research contributions of the institution. It should be interoperable so that it can be searched by search engines and other discovery tools and users outside the institution are able to find and retrieve information from the repository thus making its content available to the broader research community.

INSTITUTIONAL REPOSITORY SOFTWARES

The landscape of software platforms for building institutional repositories is constantly changing. Major features of some of the IR softwares available through open sources are described below:

- Archimede
- Bepress
- CDSware
- DSpace
- EPrints
- Fedora
- Greenstone
- Open Repository

Archimede : Developed at Laval University Library, Archimede is open source software for building institutional repositories. It has been developed with a "multilingual perspective," offering English, French and Spanish interfaces. With a focus on internationalization, the software interface is independent and not embedded in the code. This allows you to develop additional language-specific interfaces without re-coding the software itself. It also lets users switch from language to language "anywhere and anytime" while searching for and retrieving content.

bepress : Developed by the Berkeley Electronic Press, bepress builds and hosts their customers' repositories. Cost includes software, custom implementation, infrastructure, training, hosting, offsite backup, technical support, and software upgrades.

CDSware (CERN Document Server Software) : Developed by CERN, the European Organization for Nuclear Research, based in Geneva, CDSware is designed to run an electronic preprint server, online library catalogue, or a document system on the web.

DSpace : DSpace is a digital library system designed to capture, store, index, preserve, and redistributes the intellectual output of a university's research faculty in digital formats. developed jointly by HP Labs and MIT Libraries.

EPrints : GNU EPrints is free, open source software developed at the University of Southampton. It is designed to create a pre-print institutional repository for scholarly research, but can be used for other purposes.

Fedora (Flexible Extensible Digital Object and Repository Architecture) : Jointly developed by University of Virginia and Cornell University, Fedora (Flexible Extensible Digital Object Repository) serves as a foundation for building interoperable web-based digital libraries, institutional repositories, and other information management systems. It demonstrates how you can deploy a distributed digital library architecture using web-based technologies, including XML and Web services.

Greenstone : Developed by the New Zealand Digital Library Project at the University of Waikato, Greenstone is a suite of software for building and distributing digital library collections. Greenstone was developed and distributed in cooperation with UNESCO and the Human Info NGO.

Open Repository : Open Repository is a new offering from BioMed Central, providing a commercial software service for building institutional repositories. Based on the DSpace software, it offers multiple editions with varying levels of support and service.

Commercial Digital Repository Software's : Apart from the above Open Source Software, some commercially developed softwares also available for digital repository. The name of few is mentioned herein below;

CONTENTdm® : Developed at the University of Washington and distributed by OCLC. The software has tools for acquiring or creating collections; tools for storage of the content and a set of tools for display and retrieval of objects. CONTENTdm also offers scalable tools for archiving collections of any size.

Digi Tool : This is a 'enterprise solution for the management of digital assets in Libraries and academic environment.

EN Compass : It is a one module of EN Compass or suite of software for managing and accessing digital content. EN Compass has many modules for various purposes.

Hyperion : It provides organisation, storage and access to digital files by searching both associated Meta data and full text of text files.

Meta Source : Meta source is a suite of tolls used to manage digital collections, including, digital object storage, crawling external collections and support for Metadata schemes.

VITAL : VITAL is a institutional repository software

developed by VTLS. VITAL is a set of workflow extensions, management utilities and enhanced searching capabilities build on Fedora Repository Architecture.

INSTITUTIONAL REPOSITORIES AND LIBRARIES IN INDIA

A number of Indian scientific research institutions, universities and corporate R&Ds produce high quality research accompanied by innumerable scholarly communications published by national and international journals and conference proceedings. Large amount of high qualities, peer reviewed open access journals are being published by Indian scholars covering a wide spectrum of subjects. More than 50 academic and research institutions have set up their Institutional Repositories viz., IISc, IIMK, ISI, NCL, NIO, RRU, NAL, NIT and so on. Some of the institutions names are mentioned below: Documentation Research Training Centre (DRTC), Indian Institute of Astrophysics, Indian Institute of Technology, Delhi, Indian Institute of Technology, Mumbai, Indian National Science Academy (INSA), Indira Gandhi National Open University (IGNOU), Information and Library Network Centre (INFLIBNET), National Aerospace Laboratories, National Centre for Catalysis Research, National Informatics Centre (NIC), National Institute of Oceanography (NIO), Indian Institute of Management Kozhikode, Indian Statistical Institute, Library etc.

USE OF IR

Universities and research libraries around the world use institutional repository in the following ways:

- Scholarly communication
- Storing learning materials and courseware
- Electronic publishing
- Managing collections of research documents
- Preserving digital materials for the long term
- Adding to the university's prestige by showcasing its academic research

- Institutional leadership role for the Library
- Knowledge management
- Research assessment
- Encouraging open access to scholarly research
- Housing digitized collections

Each university has a unique culture and assets that require a customized approach. The information model that best suits your university would not fit another campus.

CONCLUSION

ICT has created great opportunities for the future of services provided by the learned societies. Institutional Repositories disseminate intellectual outcome of digitized materials drafted and published by those societies. IRs also provides efficiencies by removing information technology barriers. An IR also can showcase the research, teaching, and scholarship at an institutional level. In a university setting, an IR provides a centralized digital showcase through which community members can highlight their work.

REFERENCES

1. Das, A.K., B.K. Sen and Chaitali Dutta, Collection development in digital information repositories in India.
2. Crow, R. (2002). The case for institutional repositories: A SPARC position paper, ARL Bimonthly Report, vol. 223, 2002.
3. *B Lavoie*, HF Nielsen: Web characterization terminology & definitions sheet, W3C working draft 24-May-1999.
4. N. Kumar, Ashok. : Institutional Repositories in India, http://eprints.rclis.org
5. Lynch, C. A. (2003). Institutional repositories: essential infrastructure for scholarship in the digital age, ARL Bimonthly Report, vol. 226, 2003.
6. Newton, Mark P.; Miller, Christopher C.; and Bracke, Marianne S., "Librarian Roles in Institutional Repository Data Set Collecting: Outcomes of a Research Library Task Force" (2011). Libraries Research Publications. Paper 122.

7. Sarah L.Shreeves and Melissa H. Cragin, Special Issue, Library Trends 57, no 2 (Fall 2008): 191-201.

8. Witt, Michael. "Institutional Repositories and Research Data Curation in a Distributed Environment." in "Institutional Repositories: Current State and Future," eds.

9. http://contentdm.com/

10. http://www.dspace.org

11. http://www.bepress.com/repositories.htm

12. http://www1.bibl.ulaval.ca/archimede/index.en.html

13. http://www.fedora.info/index.shtml

14. http://www.greenstone.org/cgi-bin/library

15. http://www.openrepository.com/default.asp

16. http://software.eprints.org

10

Digital Preservation: It's Need, Challenges and Strategies for Preserving Digital Contents, Role of International/National Organizations

Manjula C

Library Professional, Tamil Nadu Digital Library Project, Chennai

DIGITAL PRESERVATION: IT'S NEED

Digital records preservation is one of several activities that are carried out as part of the records management function. Digital preservation is not simply a process of capturing digital records and holding them in a digital repository. It must be carried out in relation to well-run records systems. Otherwise, the records and the connections between them cannot be preserved systematically, and much of the meaning will be lost, even within a short period of time. This lesson begins, therefore, with an illustrated overview of essential records concepts before moving on to describe digital records preservation concepts. It provides the background to a discussion of digital records preservation concepts including the factors that influence the integrity of records when they stored for the long-term.

'Records' are information created, received, and maintained as evidence and information by an organization or person, in pursuance of legal obligations or in the transaction of business (*ISO 15489*); digital record: a document in digital form that is managed as a record . Records are a special form of recorded information. The fundamental role of document decision is to be action, activities and communication to tell the story as it happened. Based on their role in telling the story, records should be capable of serving multiple business purposes when they are complete and well managed.

Records provide evidence : For example, the ministry creates records of the evaluation process to show how it chooses one company instead of another.

Records support decision-making : For example, submissions are in a standard format that allows comparisons to be made between companies in terms of costs, work plans, experience, etc.

Records enable the organization to hold itself accountable : For example, the records can be used to show that the ministry has complied with procurement regulations; the records can also be used to respond to a formal request under the Freedom of Information law about the award of the contract.

Records support the pursuit of individual rights and entitlements: For example, the records can be used to defend the ministry against a company's claim that it was not fairly treated in the tendering process. Taking another example, records can be used to support tenants' claims that insufficient compensation has been paid when a building they have been living in has been demolished during a construction project.

- Records are the source of valuable data and information

for monitoring, analyzing and planning. For example, information from a contracting process is combined with information on all other contracts for construction projects in the same year; the combined information is analysed to report on how much was spent, on what types of projects, where and so on.

- In order to serve these multiple purposes, records must be capable of being related to one another. For example, records created as part of a single contracting process are linked. The records also must be reliable, authentic and accessible for as long as they are required. In records management, integrity is the term often used to describe these qualities meaning the records are whole and without corruption.

Records typically comprise *content* (what the record says), *context* (where the record comes from, how it came to be created, when and by whom) and *structure* (the different parts of the record). The records' content, context and structure must be assembled and maintained, especially if they are in digital form, to enable them to serve their purposes. The records' content, context and structure must be preserved throughout their life span; otherwise their integrity will be affected, and they may no longer have the same meaning or be understandable at all. The quality of the information extracted from the records now and overtime will depend on preserving the records' integrity.

Records are the product of work processes, also called business processes. The quality and integrity of records depend on the quality and integrity of the work processes that generate them. Clearly, if the work processes are poorly defined or inconsistent or not followed correctly, the records produced may not be adequate.

A work process is a set of related tasks. *Workflow* refers to the order in which these tasks are carried out and how. Work processes support a given function (i.e. what the organisation does). The organization's functions and processes are managed by accountable individuals. The organizational structure is, in one sense, a management structure for the organization's functions, processes and tasks. The organisation should have an accountability framework (who is responsible and accountable for what), which itself is derived from a mandate(s) and/ or an enabling law(s) or some other authority. In other words, the organization's mandate defines what it should do; the accountability framework determines who is responsible; and the processes and tasks are how it is done.

CHALLENGES TO THE PRESERVATION OF DIGITAL RECORDS

In addition to risks from viruses, the following factors need to be considered when developing strategies for preserving digital records. These issues must be addressed together as part of a unified strategy if the records are to survive and have integrity.

MEDIA FRAGILITY

Digital records are stored on a variety of media including, for example, CDs, external hard disks, floppy disks and internal disk drives. They are stored on network servers, database servers and a variety of other digital media. The common factor is that the records are stored in a digital format. Whatever the storage medium, all digital records are at risk from loss or destruction for the following reasons:

Fragility of the digital media : The life span of floppy disks (no longer made but still kept in many organizations) is three to five years; the life span of hard disks is two to eight years; and the life span of magnetic tape is 10 to 30 years.

Poor environmental storage conditions : Storage media are sensitive to extremes and changes in temperature and humidity.

Lack of available technology : For example, 5 ¼ inch diskettes can only be read by obsolete equipment.

Quality of the media : Some brands of storage media are of lower quality than others and may be more at risk.

Software and Hardware Obsolescence Continual changes to the original creating software and hardware, and the rapid obsolescence of digital technologies, have critical consequences for organizations. We can read paper documents that were written hundreds of years ago and, assuming they have been kept in reasonable storage conditions, we can see them exactly as they were when originally created. For digital records, we need completely different strategies if the records are to be read in future.

In exploring the issue of software and hardware obsolescence, it is important to understand that obsolescence can occur at different times for any one or all of the following reasons:

Computer hardware : Computers ranging from so-called mainframes to personal computers to smart phones are obsolete after only a few years of use. Many vendors of computer hardware products have disappeared taking their technology with them (eg WANG, Atari, etc).

System software : The operating systems supported by major vendors such as Apple and Microsoft can become obsolete as new versions are developed; for instance, Windows 95 is no longer supported; present-day software may not be able to run on Windows 95.

Application software : Even if the hardware and operating systems are still available, records may be at risk if the application software (for example, word processing software, spreadsheet software, etc) normally supported by the hardware and operating system no longer exist (eg MultiMate) or if so many versions have been developed that records created using earlier versions can no longer be read. There are many examples of old versions of business applications (eg for accounting or financial management systems) that are no longer supported by the vendor.

Recording formats : The hardware, operating system and application software may be in place, but if the records are recorded in a format that is not recognized, they may not be retrievable unless they are converted to another format. Some digital photo formats can only be read by certain software, and those who use Apple computers will understand the challenges that are sometimes encountered in exchanging documents and images with Microsoft PCs and vice versa.

Storage media : 5 ¼ and 3 ½ floppy disks are difficult to find today because they have been superseded by more sophisticated storage media capable of storing much larger volumes of data. With the introduction of new storage media, from flash drives to high density tapes and from disks to hard drives and servers, digital records stored on older media must be migrated to new media. Organizations are driven to upgrade their storage technologies to ensure that records continue to be accessible. However, copying from storage media to storage media has its own risks as the records may be in danger of being lost or corrupted during the process.

All of these risks to digital records must be monitored. Strategies are needed to ensure that rapidly changing technologies do not affect the integrity of digital records through time.

INADEQUATE META DATA

The companion to the training module, *Managing Meta data to Protect the Integrity of Digital Records,* describes in detail the risks associated with inadequate meta data. The purpose of meta data is to describe records in the context of their creation in a manner that facilitates access and retrieval, enables records to be understood and maintains the integrity of records through time. The risks arising when meta data are insufficient, inaccurate or incomplete are summarized as follows:

- failure to locate information
- inability to render and read the information
- lack of meaning or value in the information
- inability to verify the authenticity of information.

ROLE OF INTERNATIONAL AND NATIONAL ORGANIZATIONS

The four brief presentations that describe activities at the national level in four different countries, it is anticipated that indications of strategic overlap will begin to emerge, which may then suggest areas where an increased focus on joint international working may be appropriate.

NEIL GRINDLEY – THE JOINT INFORMATION SYSTEMS COMMITTEE (JISC) UK

The JISC is an organization that supports the innovative use of information and communications technology to support teaching and research in UK Higher and Further Education. It achieves this by: careful and selective funding of relevant programmes of work that are firstly endorsed and then overseen by representatives of the community that it serves; and by the formation of strategic partnerships and collaborations with a wide range of organisations both within and beyond the UK. The Digital Preservation and Records Management Programme is the current iteration of a long-running commitment on the part of the JISC to support institutions in keeping digital materials viable and accessible during their entire life- cycle, and incorporates a number of projects, studies and collaborative initiatives that together form the substance of the programme and deliver its benefit to the community.

MARTHA ANDERSON – LIBRARY OF CONGRESS (USA) – NATIONAL DIGITAL INFORMATION INFRASTRUCTURE AND PRESERVATION PROGRAMME (NDIIP)

Martha Anderson will introduce the Library of Congress Programme that has established a network of partners dedicated to collecting and preserving important born- digital information. This national network currently has more than 100 participating entities and has worked on: developing roles and functions for the stewardship of at- risk content; building communities of practice; developing shared services; and building capacity for digital preservation work. The stakeholders in this network represent public and private sector organisations including government agencies, commercial content producers, libraries, archives and technology entities.

STEVE KNIGHT - THE NATIONAL LIBRARY OF NEW ZEALAND

The National Library of New Zealand (Te Puna M—tauranga o Aotearoa) Act 2003 requires the National Library to collect, preserve, protect and make accessible digital collections, along with traditional paper collections, in ways that ensure current and future access to New Zealand's documentary heritage.

The National Digital Heritage Archive (NDHA) Programme was established in July 2004. Due to be completed in 2009, the NDHA is being developed and implemented in partnership with Ex Libris Group and Sun Microsystems as a commercially viable solution addressing the ingest, workflow, provenance, integrity/ authenticity etc issues of institutional digital preservation.

This presentation will outline the National Library's work on digital preservation, how the NDHA fits into that work, what is expected to be delivered through the NDHA, how the organisation is preparing to integrate the new systems, and some comment on the issues going forwards.

NATASCHA SCHUMANN – THE GERMAN NATIONAL LIBRARY

The German National Library is one of seven project partners participating in Nestor: The German Network of Expertise in Digital Long-Term Preservation. Natascha Schumann will give an overview of the benefits and the problems of cooperation among diverse communities. She will consider which synergies can be leveraged and which differences have to be taken into account. Issues such as different legal mechanisms for undertaking preservation and different terminologies across communities will be considered. Acknowledgement will also be made of the variances in priorities across disciplines for different approaches to preservation, e.g. the need for 'raw data' curation procedures within the scientific community.

INDIAN INITIATIVES TOWARDS DIGITAL PRESERVATION:

INITIATIVES IN DIGITAL PRESERVATION OF MANUSCRIPTS IN INDIA

Thinking the importance of digital preservation, in India too, numbers of projects are taken by different organizations for the preservation of these valuable manuscripts in digital format. In July 2000, a pilot project for digitization of rare manuscripts had been initiated by National Archives of India, collaboration with Department of Science and Technology and National Institute of Advanced Studies, Bangalore. Under this project, rare manuscripts, viz. Bhagwadgita, Ramayana, Mahabharata, etc. have been digitized and stored in CD medium.

One of the major functions of the National Library of a country is to collect and preserve nation's intellectual and cultural heritage. Therefore National Library has taken several steps to preserve this heritage as well as to increase the accessibility and awareness of these records. National Library of India, Kolkata is the apex body of library services India. This National Library has about 3600 rare and historically important manuscripts in different languages. These manuscripts are preserved separately in the Rare Books Division. This library has initiated a digitization programme, known as 'Down the Memory Lane', to digitize these manuscripts along with other rare books and documents, from its collection. These scanned documents are archiving on CDs. Between the year 1999 and 2001 approximately 6601 books and manuscripts containing 2.5 million pages were scanned and archived in 548 CD-ROMs.

DIGITAL LIBRARY INITIATIVES IN INDIA

During the past five years, India has seen several Digital Library initiatives at the institutional, organizational and at national levels. Some of them are quite successful while others are making significant progress.

Some of the major initiatives on Digital Libraries in India are furnished below:

- 'Archives of Indian Labour' at the V.V. Giri Institute of Labour (http://www.indialabourarchives.org/sources/jnu.htm)
- Indian Institute of Science NCSI (http://vidya-mapak.ncsi.iisc.ernet.in/cgi-bin/library)
- Indian Institute of Management Kozhikode (http://intranet.iimk.ac.in/cgi-bin/library)
- Search Digital Library SDL at DRTC Bangalore (https://drtc.isibang.ac.in/index.jsp)
- Nalanda Digital library, National Institute of Technology (NIT) Calicut (http://www.nalanda.nitc.ac.in)
- Vidyanidhi Project (http://www.vidyanidhi.org.in)
- Million Book Universal Digital library Project - Carnegie Mellon - IISc - ERNET (http://www.dli.ernet.in)
- Indira Gandhi Centre for the ARTS (IGNCA Digital Library) -(http://ignca.nic.in)
- INDEST, Ministry of HRD, GOI (http://paniit.iitd.ac.in/indest)
- National Tuberculosis Institute (NTI), Bangalore (http://ntiindia.kar.nic.in/)
- Rajiv Gandhi University of Health Sciences, Karnataka (RGUHS) http://www.rguhs.ac.in/dl/index.html)
- Traditional Knowledge Digital Library (TKDL) – (http://203.200.90.6/tkdl/langdefault/common/home.asp)
- Indian School of Business (http://www.isb.edu/lrc/index.html)
- Indian Institute of Technology, Kharagpur (http://www.library.iitkgp.ernet.in/usr/elib/digital.htm)
- Indian Institute of Technology, Mumbai (http://www.library.iitb.ac.in/~mnj/gsdl/cgi-bin/library)
- IITMK Trivandrum (http://www.iiitmk.ac.in/iiitmk/digitallibrary.htm)

- National Chemical Laboratory (NCL, CSIR) - Digital Repository – (http://dspace.ncl.res.in)
- University of Hyderabad (http://202.41.85.234:8000/cgi-bin/gw_42_6/chameleon

PROBLEMS ASSOCIATED WITH DIGITAL LIBRARIES – POSSIBLE SOLUTIONS

The digitization initiatives in India are encountered with the problems of lack of technical infrastructure, trained manpower, finances and policy initiatives. Some of the problems are:-

(a) Lack of clear cut policy at National level with main focus on sustainability

(b) Outdated software and hardware and difficulty in upgrading the same.

(c) Non-availability of cost effective new technological advancement.

(d) Lack of multiple Indian language OCR facilities.

(e) Non-standard technical activities, data description and transmission characteristics.

(f) Non-availability of well-trained skilled personnel.

(g) Lack of management support

(h) Lack of proper preservation policy

(i) No Intellectual Property Rights policy for content development of digital information.

(j) Rigidity in the publishers' policies and data formats

The above factors affect the success of digitization initiatives and the creation of digital libraries. These problems have to be addressed positively to ensure planned digital resource development programmes and digital libraries in the country. In order to achieve it, the following factors may be taken into consideration.

NATIONAL POLICY FOR DIGITIZATION – SHOULD FOCUS ON

- Education and life long learning for all citizens
- Information to enhance participation of citizens in the socio-economic development
- Promotion of business and economy, training and employment
- Traditional knowledge and preservation of cultural heritage
- Developing repository of historical evidence and community history

SUSTAINABILITY ISSUES

For issues related to sustainability, the main focus will have to be on the following areas:

- user focused Policy and Strategies
- provision for refreshing the data
- user charges, prices, framing guidelines for fixation of prices,
- people's participation, Political and administrative will,
- capacity building to develop skilled man power,
- co-operative subscriptions, shared technology system, resource sharing, joint archives
- 1changing role of librarians and information professionals

DIGITAL DIVIDE

The major issues to be addressed in India before taking initiatives to create the digital libraries are:-

- Creation of basic infrastructural facilities such as internet and telecommunications etc.
- Creation of awareness among the users on usage of technology.

REFERENCE

Arts and Humanities Data Service (AHDS). AHDS Repository Policies and Procedures.

Digital Preservation Coalition 2014 – and Amy Kirchhoff and Sheila M. Morrissey 2014. DOI: http://dx.doi.org/10.7207/twr14-01

https://www.dpconline.org/docs/digital-preservation-handbook/299-digital-preservation-handbook/file

http://www.bic.org.uk/files/pdfs/digpres.pdf

11

Cloud Computing – An Overview

V.Senthur Velmurugan

M.A., M.L.I.SC., M.PHIL. (P.HD), Librarian, n- CARDMATH,

Kalasalingam Academy of Research and Education,

(Deemed to be University) Krishnankovil- 626 126. Tamilnadu, India.

ABSTRACT

Distributed computing has grown up since Amazon's rollout of the first of its sort of cloud benefits in 2006. It is especially important to Hong Kong as a result of the gigantic measures of information that are being handled here day by day in different divisions, and there are signs that membership to cloud benefits by the nearby organizations will soon be on a skyrocket course, regardless of a moderate begin in earlier years. The expression "distributed computing" is a current trendy expression in the IT world. Behind this favor idyllic expression there lays a genuine photo without bounds of processing for both in specialized viewpoint and social point of view. Despite the fact that the expression "Distributed computing" is later however concentrating calculation and capacity in circulated server farms kept up by outsider organizations isn't new yet it returned in path in 1990s alongside dispersed registering approaches like framework processing. Distributed computing is gone for giving IT as a support of the cloud client's on-request premise with more prominent ûexibility, accessibility, dependability and adaptability with utility registering model.

Keywords : Cloud computing, cloud security, cloud service provider, SaaS, PaaS and IaaS.

INTRODUCTION

Distributed computing comprises of three particular sorts of figuring administrations conveyed remotely to customers by means of the web. Customers regularly pay a month to month or yearly administration charge to suppliers, to access frameworks that convey programming as an administration, stages as an administration and foundation as an administration to endorsers. Customers who buy in to distribute computing administrations can receive an assortment of rewards, contingent upon their specific business needs at a given point in time. The times of vast capital interests in programming and IT framework are presently a relic of days gone by for any venture that embraces the distributed computing model for obtainment of IT administrations.

WHAT IS CLOUD COMPUTING

In distributed computing, the capital interest in building and keeping up server farms is supplanted by expending IT assets as a versatile, utility-like administration from a cloud "supplier" (counting stockpiling, registering, organizing, information preparing and examination, application advancement, machine learning, and even completely oversaw administrations). Though in the past distributed computing was viewed as the territory of new businesses and forcefully visionary undertaking clients, today, it is a piece of the venture processing standard over each industry, for associations of any kind and size.

TOP BENEFITS OF CLOUD COMPUTING

Distributed computing is a major move from the customary way organizations consider IT assets. What is it about distributed computing? Why is distributed computing so well known? Here are 6 normal reasons associations are swinging to distributed computing administrations:

1. Cost

Distributed computing wipes out the capital cost of purchasing equipment and programming and setting up and running nearby datacenters—the racks of servers, the round-the-clock power for power and cooling, the IT specialists for dealing with the foundation. It includes quick.

2. Speed

Most distributed computing administrations are given self administration and on request, so even huge measures of processing assets can be provisioned in minutes, normally with only a couple of mouse clicks, giving organizations a great deal of adaptability and taking the weight off scope organization

3. Worldwide scale

The advantages of distributed computing administrations incorporate the capacity to scale flexibly. In cloud talk, that implies conveying its perfect measure assets—for instance, pretty much processing power, stockpiling, data transfer capacity—right when its required and from the privilege geographic area.

4. Unwavering quality

Distributed computing makes information reinforcement, debacle recuperation and business progression less demanding and more affordable, on the grounds that information can be reflected at different excess destinations on the cloud supplier's system.

5. Efficiency

On location datacenters normally require a considerable measure of "racking and stacking"— equipment set up, programming fixing and other tedious IT administration errands. Distributed computing expels the requirement for a large number of these undertakings, so IT groups can invest energy in accomplishing more imperative business objectives.

6. Execution

The greatest distributed computing administrations keep running on an overall system of secure datacenters, which are frequently moved up to the most recent age of quick and proficient figuring equipment. This offers a few advantages over a solitary corporate datacenter, including decreased system inactivity for applications and more noteworthy economies of scale.

COMMON CLOUD SERVICE MODELS

Cloud administrations are ordinarily sent in light of the end-client (business) prerequisites. The essential administrations incorporate the accompanying:

1. Programming as a Service (SaaS)

SaaS is a product conveyance strategy that gives access to programming and its capacities remotely as a Web-based administration. Rather than paying a forthright expense to buy as well as permit programming, SaaS clients pay a repeating (regularly month to month or yearly) charge to buy in to the administration. As a rule, they can get to the SaaS from any Internet-associated gadget, whenever day or night. Surely understood cases of SaaS incorporate Salesforce.com, Microsoft Office 365, Google G Suite, Dropbox, Adobe Creative Cloud and others.

The advantages of SaaS

- You can join and quickly begin utilizing creative business applications
- Apps and information are open from any associated PC
- No information is lost if your PC breaks, as information is in the cloud
- The benefit can progressively scale to use needs

2. Stage as a Service (PaaS)

PaaS is a registering stage being conveyed as an

administration. Here the stage is outsourced set up of an organization or server farm obtaining and dealing with its own particular equipment and programming layers. Most PaaSes are intended for designers and plan to improve the way toward making and conveying programming. For instance, a Web engineer may utilize a PaaS that incorporates working framework programming, Web server programming, a database and related Web improvement instruments. The main PaaS merchants incorporate Amazon Web Services, Microsoft Azure, IBM and Google Cloud Platform.

The advantages of PaaS

- Develop applications and get the chance to showcase speedier
- Deploy new web applications to the cloud in minutes
- Reduce many-sided quality with middleware as an administration

3. Foundation as a Service (IaaS)

PC foundation, for example, servers, stockpiling and systems administration conveyed as an administration. IaaS is well known with undertakings that value the comfort of having the cloud seller deal with their IT framework. They additionally at times observe cost reserve funds because of paying just for the processing assets they utilize. The main IaaS merchants incorporate Amazon Web Services, Microsoft Azure, IBM and Google Cloud Platform.

While SaaS, PaaS and IaaS are the three most normal sorts of cloud administrations, distributed computing sellers now and again additionally utilize other "as an administration" names to depict their offerings. For instance, some offer database as an administration (DBaaS), portable back-end as an administration (MBaaS), works as an administration (FaaS) or others.

The advantages of IaaS

- No need to put resources into your own equipment

- Infrastructure scales on request to help dynamic workloads
- Flexible, imaginative administrations accessible on request

TYPES OF CLOUD COMPUTING

There are 3 major sending models of distributed computing; open cloud, private cloud and crossover cloud.

1. Open Cloud

An open cloud is the place administrations and foundation are facilitated off-webpage by a cloud supplier, shared over their customer base and got to by these customers by means of open systems, for example, the web. Open mists offer incredible economies of scale and repetition yet are more helpless than private cloud setups due their abnormal amounts of availability.

2. Private Cloud

Private mists utilize pooled administrations and foundation put away and kept up on a private system – whether physical or virtual – available by just a single customer. The conspicuous advantages to this are more noteworthy levels of security and control. Money saving advantages must be relinquished to some degree however, as the undertaking being referred to should buy/lease and keep up all the important programming and equipment.

3. Half and half Cloud

As the name recommends, a half breed cloud consolidates both open and private cloud components. A cross breed cloud enables an organization to amplify their efficiencies; by using people in general cloud for non-delicate activities while utilizing a private setup for touchy or mission basic tasks, organizations can guarantee that their figuring setup is perfect without paying any more than is important.

CHARACTERISTICS OF CLOUD COMPUTING

The basic attributes can be expounded as takes after:

1. On-request self-benefit

Clients can arrangement distributed computing assets without requiring human association, for the most part done however an electronic self-benefit gateway (administration support).

2. Wide system gets to

Distributed computing assets are available over the system, supporting heterogeneous customer stages, for example, cell phones and workstations.

3. Asset pooling

Administration various clients from the same physical assets, by safely isolating the assets on consistent level.

4. Fast flexibility

Assets are provisioned and discharged on-request and additionally robotized in light of triggers or parameters. This will ensure your application will have precisely the limit it needs anytime of time.

5. Estimated benefit

Asset use are observed, estimated, and announced (charged) straightforwardly in view of usage. To put it plainly, pay for utilize.

As we see, distributed computing is considerably more than just virtualization. It's extremely about using innovation "as an administration". Clients require next to zero information on the subtle elements of how a specific administration is actualized, on which equipment, on what number of CPU's, et cetera. All that is vital for a client is to have great comprehension of what the administration offers—and what it doesn't—and how to work the self-benefit entryway.

CONCLUSION

Taking everything into account, distributed computing is as of late new innovative improvement that can possibly greatly affect the world. It has numerous advantages that it gives to its clients and organizations. For instance, a portion of the advantages that it gives to organizations is that it diminishes working expense by spending less on support and programming redesigns and concentrates more on the organizations itself. Be that as it may, there are different difficulties the distributed computing must overcome. Individuals are extremely incredulous about whether their information is secure and private. There are no guidelines or directions overall gave information through distributed computing. Europe has information security laws yet the US, being a standout amongst the most innovative propels country, does not have any information insurance laws. Clients likewise stress over who can uncover their information and have responsibility for information. Be that as it may, once, there are benchmarks and direction around the world, distributed computing will reform what's to come.

REFERENCE

1. https://azure.microsoft.com/en-in/overview/what-is-cloud-computing/
2. https://www.webopedia.com/TERM/C/cloud_computing.html
3. https://www.ibm.com/cloud/learn/what-is-cloud-computing
4. https://apprenda.com/library/cloud/introduction-to-cloud-computing/
5. https://cloud.google.com/what-is-cloud-computing/
6. https://www.interoute.com/what-cloud-computing
7. https://sites.google.com/site/cloudcomputingfuture/home/conclusion
8. https://www.ibm.com/blogs/cloud-computing/2014/01/31/cloud-computing-defined-characteristics-service-levels/

12

Marketing of Information Services and Products in Library and Information Centers: Application of Social Media

Bilal Ahmad Dar
Librarian, Department of Education, Govt. of J&K
Shabir Ahmad
Librarian, Department of Education, Govt. of J&K

ABSTRACT

Libraries and Information Centers and Systems have traditionally been engaged in acquiring, collecting processing, filtering and dissemination and use of information products and services .Library and information's centers are social and services oriented Institutions and have acquired a moral obligation of information services and consultations towards the society. Libraries and information centers are treasure house of human knowledge. The holdings of libraries and archives are the price less heritage of civilization has to be accessed and harnessed for human development and growth. This is possible through the marketing of information services and products supported and promoted by libraries and information centers. The chapter discusses the broader issue of Marketing perspective purpose, need and recent trends of marketing of information products which need to be employed by the libraries for proper and timely utilization of library services and products.

Keywords : Library and Information Centers (LICs), Marketing, Information Services, Information Products, Social Networking Sites, Facebook, Twitter, LinkedIn etc.

1. INTRODUCTION

Libraries are among other things, the conservation of civilization. The libraries and information systems (LIS) of different Hues that have existed from a long past to support and promote access to information and services , offer ample evidence to the fact ,that libraries are very crucial and indispensable for the social-economic development of the society . Libraries and information systems identify, acquire, preserve and provide access to the world's published knowledge (Hiremath,C.V,and Karisiddappa, C.R 2000). Historically libraries of all types have been providing a meaningful structure for collection, organization and accessing of information to facilitate accomplishment of all enterprises in which the social beings have been engaged world wide. These libraries and the information Systems would professionally select and acquire Information sources, organize them with a unique professional mechanism and make them available to these who needed them (Dar and Naikoo, 2017).

Libraries and information centre are facing a time of extraordinary change as well as challenges (Gupta,2003) These changes can be attributed to the impact of technology , new methods of information provision and declining library budgets (Sharma and Bhardwaj, 2009 Information and Communication Technologies (ICTS) have influenced the nature of business and management of libraries . Libraries are undergoing significant changes today in the outlook, function services, methods and Techniques for collection development processing and dissemination of information (Singh and Krishna, as cited in Kanamadi of Kumbar, 2006). Information technology has created a new gate way for information services. the networking demands, competition by data base vendors, and complexity in information requirements have contributed in forcing information professionals to adopt marketing so as to improve the management of library and information centers (Madhusudhan, 2008) Recent technological developments are creating forms of information and new sources of information and new ways of providing information that seems to bypass traditional institutions like libraries. Changes in technical and technological aspects of library services and products have compelled library professionals to market their services and products for increasing its visibility, providing quality services and also for fulfilling the organizational objectives. In the contemporary world, irrespective of the kind of library, it has been very essential to market the library services and products to enhance the awareness among the user community.

2. MARKETING CONCEPT DEFINED

The term marketing has many meanings, depending on the discipline and the area in which term is being used. "Marketing's planning and managing the organization's exchange relations with its clientele. It consists of studying the target market's needs, designing appropriate products and services and using effective pricing, communication, and distribution to inform, motivate, and serve the market" (Jestin and Parameshwari, 2002, p.2). Marketing is a comprehensive term and it is very important to clarify what marketing means in the library and information science. The term is related to the marketing of information and the promotion of library services, "Marketing is not so much about selling information products to researchers, as it is more about spreading the word about potentially useful new tools, it is also keeping users informed about library activities and involving them in the collection development" (Noel and Waugh, 2002, p.2). Gupta, 2006, describes the term in relation to several points, "Establishing relationships with users, providing information services and competing with others, using the internet to provide services and to reach their users". Marketing also helps to contribute to building a relationship with the users that begins and end with awareness (Kaur, 2009)

Marketing is a method or a pragmatic action through which the commodities are promoted and the diffused to the consumers. It has a special meaning in terms of library services as the core product of library is 'information' a marketable good and is intangible in nature though considered to possess the qualities of any given commodities (Gireesh, T.K and Kumar, 2013). This study defines the term, 'library marketing' as the distribution and provision of awareness of the existence of the library, and its resources and services, using different tools and technologies in order to get users to use these resources and services. It is about reaching the user and informing them of library services and activities by using existing technologies that fit in with user's needs in the new era (Salim Alkindi and Mohammed Nasser Al-Suqri, 2013)

3. MARKETING CONCEPT IN THE LIBRARY AND INFORMATION SYSTEM

The concept of marketing is not restricted only to profit making organizations .Researchers believe that marketing is relevant and also beneficial to the library Environment Marketing in its library sense refers to the instruments through which information (whether raw or processed) is transmitted to its members (Kerdadamath, N. D) Kotlar (cited in Kendadamath, N.D) is of the opinion that marketing can be equally applied to non-profit organizations as well as to colleges, universities ,charitable institutions, libraries , information centers and services organizations of all kinds,(Gupta, 2003) believes that marketing provides an opportunity that leads one to see how effective and efficient services can be offered to their users or customers.

Information professionals believe that the marketing of information has been a popular topic in the library profession in recent years. Marketing of information services has to do with the transference of information to the potential user/customer.

In the beginning of marketing concept of library and information services(LIS),some information professionals were of the opinion that marketing of library products and services is not possible in the profession of librarian ship in the sense that library is not profit -making profession . With the change in information need, its explosion, different formats of information packing and dissemination, the perception and attitude of information professionals also changed viz-a-viz marketing of library information services (LIS). Library and information products and services are now being seen as products which can be sold ,exchanged ,lent, and transmitted Therefore ,the concept of marketing in LIS has been perceived as a comprehensive term that explains all the processes and interactions that result in the satisfaction of the users and the revenue it brings for the information organization (Madhusudhan, 2008).The aims of marketing in lis are to identify the client's base , determine and fill its needs, wants and demands which could be achieved by designing and delivering appropriate products and services, (Munshi, 2009). Gupta and Savard, 2010, convey the idea that without a marketing orientation in LIS, a high -tech library or information service would not necessarily be successful. Libraries and information centers have began to see that the concept of marketing of information products and services is essential in order to improve user satisfaction and promote the services by current and potential users' .With the increased competition in the world of information, marketing is a factor for survival, (Jestin and Parameswari, 2002). Thus, marketing in the library and information services is usually important for Libraries and Information centers to live and survive.

4. WHY MARKETING OF LIBRARY AND INFORMATION SERVICES

Librarians and the information professional constantly debate and recognize the importance of marketing and have come up with new strategies to market their services and products. Traditionally, marketing was primarily done to promote information services and other resources in order to ensure their optimum usage. Today technology has endowed information seekers with varied option to satisfy their information needs. Libraries no longer have the traditional monopoly of being the only information providers, new technologies have confronted librarians and information professionals with a huge challenge to survive and thrive in this digital age, where user community can access online information resources at any time of the day from where ever they are. Therefore all types of libraries and information centers need to marketed more than ever before (Priti Jain, 2013) To effectively reach this broadened group of potential users, it is imperative that information professionals develop positive attitudes towards marketing and that they should make it to be part of the organizational culture of libraries . Kendadamath N.D, claims that marketing is useful to university libraries because it will help in the improving the library's image and also attract more users. It will assist librarians to improve their reputation within their organization and as a profession within the society. Sharma and Bhardwaj, (2009) observe that the library has many products and services that it can market.

Marketing of information services is very essential to today's society. This is due to the fact that a society that generates and consumers the most knowledge and information is considered to be the strongest society, (Jestin and Parameswari, 2002). Gupta, 2003, contends that the real challenge for library and information professionals is not how to manage the collection, staff and technology, but how to turn these resources into services, effective marketing can increase the uses of services help training customers and non-customers as well as change users perceptions and ideas, thereby promoting the reputation of the library and its staff (Steadily, 2003). Though recent concept, marketing of LIS has emerged as new indispensable instruments in the library and information industry. It has been accepted that library and information centers have for a very long time suffered from their image and visibility problems. So, marketing of the library services has been emerged as an important area for the libraries and the information centers .This is probably why many librarians and archivists now see marketing of library services as a very important topic .Marketing plan of LIS, needs to be developed and implemented with ongoing enhancement of the services and products should follow, (Sharma and Bhardwaj, 2009)

Thus marketing is an integral part of any library and one of the best ways to enhance the use of library services and products, sophisticated marketing enriches the use of libraries and thereby archive the organizational objectives.

Marketing may be instrumental in maximizing the utilization of information products for which information centers have been investing huge amount of money, manpower and time, Communication, visibility and customers' orientation are key factors in a successful marketing.

5. RECENT TRENDS AND INNOVATION IN MARKETING OF LIS

Traditional marketing was wearisome and costly, in terms of time and money both. This has evolved into online marketing, which is both time and cost-effective. Through social media, every librarian can connect straight away with their community using a range of social media channels (Du Toit and Mulatiningisth, 2013). Effectively marketing can be done by looking at digital world requirements, understanding users' needs and behavior, and their expectations when dealing with these technologies, ICTS, has brought many advantages that can be used for innovative marketing techniques .The horizon of library marketing strategies has developed.

From library home page to social media applications due

to the revolutionary changes in the information society, Social networking technologies are new means for libraries to market their product and services to a great extent, (Majaro, 1993). Information at your door step is now changing its paradigm to bring library promotional activities at social web pages where even the library catalogue can be browsed. Social media is gaining increasing focus and it is undisputed that SNS (Social Networking Sites) such as LinkedIn, Facebook, WhatsApp and Twitter are the most visited places by the users for their updates. The transient society is a moving wheel that is heading towards digital environment where virtual libraries are gaining more importance with web based services. The applications of web 2.0 have been incorporated into library environment as library 2.0 which has brought revolutionary change in information business Library and information centers, with the use of these social media have been successfully exploiting these applications for the process of information exchange. As Mishra, 2010, denotes, librarians and information professionals must integrate web 2.0 to effectively market and advertise their services for competition for customers, competition for resources, maintain relevance, promote an updated image, visibility, valuable community resource, rising expectations and survival.

6. SOCIAL MEDIA AND: THE WAY FORWARD

The application of social media to marketing of library and information services has been described as the way of advertising library, its brand product and services via web 2.0 technologies. In using the social media tools in marketing the library services, libraries can engage with their clienteles and enable them to participate in the production of library products, (Tuten, 2001). Social media usage in marketing of library services, according Navik and Amin, 2011, enables the library to keep in constant touch with the users. Oxford Dictionary, 2013, defines s social media as, "websites and applications that enable users to create and share content or to participate in social networking". According to Bradley, 2012, the term social media refers to, "the use of web –based and mobile technologies to turn communication into an interactive dialogue". The following table provides a clear picture of advantages and revolutionary changes that social media has brought into the marketing world of library and information service:

Table 1. Traditional verses social media marketing. Courtesy: European Journal of Business, Economics and Accountancy. Vol. 1 No. 1, 2013

Traditional Marketing	Social Media Marketing
• Time consuming	• Time saving
• Expensive	• Cost-effective
• Monotonous	• Exciting and stimulating
• Limitation to reach the community	• Reachable to the community
• Static	• Creative instantly
• Limited means for marketing	• A range of social media channels for marketing
• Allows little or no interaction with user community	• Brings librarians closer to users and vice –versa
• One-way	• Collaborative
• Passive	• Interactive
• Time –bound	• No. time limitation.

7. MOST WIDELY USED SOCIAL MEDIA PLATFORMS FOR MARKETING OF LIBRARY AND INFORMATION SERVICES AND PRODUCTS

Social media platform are boon for library professional to market and publicize their services and products. They act as an online marketing tool for marketing of traditional library and information services feasibly widely. Social media provides more opportunities to reach the user community, target specific audience and give users a chance to interact with library. Statistics of the social media usage in libraries shows that there are nearly 700 million active Facebook users, over 100 million LinkedIn members 5 billion +images on Flicker, 24 million pages on

Wikipedia, 300 million twitter users posting over 7,000 tweets per second, over 2.9 billion hours of you tube watching per month (Tortorella, 2012). In marketing library and information services, the most widely used social media platforms are:

Facebook : Facebook is the most popular social media platform for creating library awareness and marketing (Chu and Do, 2013) It is the most popular tool of marketing Now -a –days, because it is librarian –friendly, Librarians can interact with users to know their information need. Libraries try to link various specialized services and applications like information absent grey literature, attention to useful hidden treasure of the library, library events and others to their Facebook pages. Photos, notes about conferences /seminars /workshop can be uploaded on the dedicated Facebook page of the library and information centers.

LinkedIn : This platform enables patterns to connect with subject specialists in their particular field of interest, library professional can use this platform to render specialized services such as selective dissemination of information (SDI) Current awareness services (CAS) document delivery services (DDS) and others. LinkedIn can be in effective marketing channel with proper planning and implementation, through the use of LinkedIn, libraries can also solicit their ideas and professional experiences.

Twitter : Twitter is the second most popular social media platform that is being used as marketing tool for LIS. It is micro-blogging network of real post and all the post are limited to 140 characters and less .It has become an increasing popular social networking tools libraries and information centers to reach out to their patrons, (Sewell, 2013). It helps to keep staff and users informed of the events and programs of library, workshop, new arrivals and new services. Marketing activities happen at its best way as it facilitates the real time communication which can also be instrumental in online reference service. Twitter can create library service alerts (Ezeani and Igwesi, 2012). Modern libraries are finding exemplary marketing strategies to engage with their followers on that is resulting in increased number of patrons twitter posts can be linked to the homepage of the library, blog posts, Wiki online archives for detailed information.

Blogs/Weblogs : A blog also called a weblog is a website consisting of entries (posts) appearing in reverse chronological order with the most recent entry appearing first. Blogs are one of the oldest social media channels. They are popularly used in libraries and information centers to broadcast library news and market other library resources, (Gunelius, 2014). Librarians can also develop subject -specific Blogs and play a leading role in advocating the Blogs for scholarly communication and commenting on research finds increasing Libraries are using Blogs for publishing library news and events, providing information about new acquisitions, and encouraging use of library services (Walia and Gupta, 2012). The Blogs are an invaluable part of New York public libraries social content marketing. Similar strategies can be incorporated in Indian Library and Information Services. All the types of library and information services, SDI, CAS, DDS, Book Reviews, and Library Events etc can be marketed through good managed library Blog.

YouTube : Libraries can market their different programs conferences and workshops by uploading the videos on the YouTube. Video clippings of documentary films of libraries and information centers give users a grid view of intact collection and environment of the library. Library products such as e-learning tutorials are promoted through virtual tour.

Flicker : Librarians can use this tool to share and distribute new images of library collections. Cover pages of new arrivals of both books and journals can be disseminated to users via flicker. Academic events such as Seminars, workshops and conference through images may be marketed to users for the awareness.

Pinterest : Pinterest is a free, graphical and an emerging social media tool. Pinterest provides great venues to market library resources. A library can make its own profile and create boards Pinning photos and video, showcasing the library (Gallardo, 2013).

The Westerville library (Unexpected Library Marketing, and Quotes About Reading) and New York took Public library are using pinterest to market library events, library collection, library educational resources (DVDS) etc.

Slide share : It is a platform for slide hosting service. Slide share has been playing a vital role in the field of marketing of education and e-learning. Sharing ideas, conducting research, connecting with others have been much effective through Slide share. Presenting prepared slides that contain information about library products and services will notify every user who visits and shares.

Others : There are other platforms of marketing in current information society. Wikis, podcasts, vodocasting, RSS feeds, Ming, MySpace etc. are innovation means which are being used for marketing of library and information service in developed world and can be employed in our country for the same.

8. CONCLUSION AND SUGGESTIONS

Library and Information Centers ought to change according to changing nature of Information and Communication Technologies to promote their services and products to maximize the utility. Responsibility of the library professionals dwells in implementing the appropriate marketing strategies using social networking technologies. Marketing policy of library and information centers using latest social media platforms needs attention while planning, structuring and execution and should be reviewed frequently with the feedback from the users. Exchange of innovative marketing proposals and experience is possible among the professional contacts if social media is effectively used. The chapter explored the concept of marketing in library and information services, need and recent trends in marketing that are being employed by both developed as well as developing countries in marketing the LIS of library and information centers. The resent experiment of social media platforms as well –recognized and well –accepted platforms for marketing of library and information service. The phenomenon of social media tools is likely to continue evolving rapidly and so should be library marketing strategies, (Chu and Du, 2013). Today libraries and information centers are using the latest technologies and trends to make their services popular and user friendly. Now, the concept of library as physical place is rapidly changing to a social cyber space where users access, communicate and contribute to existing knowledge. Today libraries and information organizations have to act as a powerful magnet in attracting the users. Thus, marketing is the way forward in transforming libraries for the future (Malik, 2009).Hence ,it is recommended that library and information centers should focus an interactive, collaborative and multi –media web –based technologies to 'web-base' library services and collections to satisfy the customer. More ever, librarians and information professionals should learn to effectively market and advertise their service for competition for customers promote updated image of their library and themselves, and maintain relevance.

REFERENCE

1. Alkindi,S.A., & Al-Sugri, Mohammad Nasser. (2013). Social networking sites as marketing and outreach tools of library and information services. Global Journal of Human Social Science, Arts, Humanities and Psychology, 13(2), 1-14.
2. Chu, S. Kai-Wah, & Du, H.S. (2013). Social networking tools for academic libraries. Journal of Librarianship and Information Science, 45(1), 64-75.
3. Dar,B.A., & Naikoo, Shabir. (2017). *Recent trends in digital archiving and preservation: A global perspective (first ed.)*. Hillsborough St, United States: Lulu Publications, pp 21.
4. Du Toit, K., & Mulatiningsih, B. (2013). Social media for libraries, Retrieved at *http://www.slideshare.net/kerendtiot/social-media–for–libraries–karen-du-toit-2692013*
5. Ezeani, C.N., & Igweshi,U. (2012). Using Social Media for Dynamic Library Service Delivery: The Nigeria experience. Library Philosophy and Practice. Retrieved on *http://www,digital.com-mens.unl.edu/libphilprac/814.*
6. Gupta, D., & Kand Savard, R. (2010). Marketing library and information

services. Retrieved at *http://mapageweb.umontreal.ca/savardr/pdf/gupta-savard-Elisbis.pdf* .

7. Gunelius, S. (2014). What is a blog? Retrieved at *http://webblogs.about.com/od/starting blog/what is a blog.htm* .

8. Gupta, D.K. (2003). Marketing of library and information services building a new discipline for library and information science education in Asia. Malaysia Journal of Library and Information Science, 8(2), 95-108

9. Hiremath, C.V., & Karisiddappa, C.R. (2000). Marketing of library and information service, concepts, issues and strategies. Dr S.R Ranganathan Memorial National Seminar 9-12th August, at Goa University.

10. Jain, Priti. (2013). Application of social media in marketing library of information services: A global perspective. European journal of Business, Economics and Accountancy, 1(1) 1-9.

11. Jestin, J.K.J., & Parameshwari, B. (2002). Marketing of information products and practice, Library Philosophy and Practice, 5(1). Retrieved at *http://www.webpages.uidaho.edu/mbolin/jestin2.pdf*

12. Kanamadi, S., & Kumbar, D.B. (2006). Web-based services expected from libraries: A case study of management institutes in Mumbai City. Webology, 3(2). Retrieved at http://*www.webology*.org/2006/v3n2/926.html

13. Kour K. (2009). Marketing the academic library on the web library management, 30(6/7), 454-468.

14. Kendadamath, G. C. (n.d). Marketing of library and information services. Retrieved at http://*www.bhu.ac.in/institute of agricaltural sciencesBHU/EXTENSIONAL-EDUCATION/WINTER/20*

15. Madhusudhaan, M. (2008). Marketing of library and I information services and products in university library. A case study of Goa University libraries. Library Philosophy and Practice. Retrieved at *http://digitalcommons.unl.edu/libphilprac/175.*

16. Majaro, S. (1993). *The essence of marketing. Englewood Cliffs.* N.J: Practice –Hall, pp-10.

17. Mishra, C.S. (2010). Marketing library and information services on the Greco Road of web 2.0. The Library Perspective Technological, 7th Convection PLANNER-2010, Tezpur University, Assam February, 10-20.

18. Munshi, N. (2009). Marketing of information services: A conceptual framework. Information Science. Retrieved at *http://www.infosciencetoday.org.*

19. Murli, N., & Gireesh Kumar, T.K. (2013). Marketing of library services and products through social media: An evaluation in national conference on inspiring library services, 2013, (NCILS-2013). Sree Siddartha Pre University College, Tumkeer, Karnataka, July 12-13.

20. Malik, F.A. (2009). Push to pull. IFLA ALP Course on information literacy. Wellington New Zealand, IFLA Asia and Oceania Section News letter 21 (C ID), 21.

21. Noel, R., & Waugh, T. (2002). Marketing library and information services: Comparing experience at large institutes in Putting Knowledge to work. Presented at the Special Libraries Association Conference, LOS, Angels California.

22. Navik, V., & Amin, J. (2011). Effective use of social media tools for marketing of library and information products and services: Facebook, Twitter and Wikipedia. Retrieved at *http://www.iimahd.ernet.in/library/PDFs/conf/002/20 viral-jignesh.pdf* .

23. Oxford Dictionary. (2013). Definition of social media in english. Retrieved at *http://www.oxforddictionaries.com/difinition/english.social-media*.

24. Sharma, A.K., & Bhardwaj.S. (2009).Marketing and promotion of library services. Retrieved at *http://ual.du.ac.in/ical09/Papers/india–files/ical-79-73-172-RV.pdf* .

25. Swell, R, R. (2013). Who is following us? Data mining on library's twitter followers. Library Hi-Tech, 31CD, 160-170.

26. Steadly, M. (2003). Marketing: The power of 10.UI current LIS clips, library and information services marketing. Retrieved at *http://www.lis.uiuc.edu/clips /2003-09.html*.

27. Tortorella, D. (2012). Library marketing and promotion via social media. Retrieved at *http://infopeople.org/training/library-marketing-ad-promotion-social-media*

28. Walia, P.K., & Gupta, M. (2012). Application of web 2.0 tools by national libraries. Webology, 9(2). Retrieved at *http://www.webology.org/2012/v9n2/a99,html*.

13

Learning Experiences of Users in Digital Era : An Overview

Sumaira Jabeen
Irfan-ul haq Akhoon
Shabir Hussain
Research scholars, Department of Library and Information science, University of Kashmir

ABSTRACT

In the present era of information and communication technology wherein knowledge is expanding exponentially. Learning is fundamental to the progress of humanity. Which can be enhanced with the help of new technologies. These (technologies) increase possibilities for learning throughout life, improve access, and spread the process of knowledge creation. Although it is difficult to keep up with this phenomenon. With the result information is not being used properly for solving the problems. There should be proper strategies which can help users to improve the abilities for problem solving. The present study is an attempt to provide an insight and awareness into the importance of learning in the society (users, education) to develop capabilities, thinking skills to solve problems according to the best of their knowledge. Which will get enhanced through the experiences they gain during their search for information associated with their tasks. Furthermore to know how can academic libraries keep up with user expectations.

Keywords : Information, Learning, Education, Experiences, Technology.

INTRODUCTION

The human skills, appreciations, reasoning, as well as human hopes , attitudes, and values are generally recognized to depend for their development largely on the events called learning (Gagne, 1970). As learning is considered at the heart of perception, thinking, imagination, reasoning, judgments, attitudes personality traits, systems of value. Thus, the development and organization of the activities that constitute personality of the individual depends on it. Infact, when a learner (person) interacts with, or is stimulated by, an environment. Others adopt the same human adaptation process acccording to (Lewin, 1951). Although experience plays a key role in the process. Even Myers (1993) defined learning as a relatively permanent change in an organism's behaviour due to experience. Kolb (1984) defined learning as a human adaptation process. It is a process whereby knowledge is created through the transformation of experience. Besides this Webster Dictionary provided common usage of the word LEARN as "to gain knowledge or understanding or skill by study, instruction, or experience". The word "gain" implies addition of new knowledge. On the other hand, "TO STUDY" can be defined as to learn or gain knowledge by means of books, observation, or experiment. To experience is to live through something, to act, to do, to respect, to suffer the consequences of, to feel, to internalize something. Could be the act of studying. Meanwhile, experiencing may involve studying but it is unlikely that studying. Yet studying has a speculative aspect to it that transcends experience in some way. The process speaks to a way of learning or thinking that is unique. The purposes for which study is intended determine its utility. Mostly the object of one's study may have no universal appeal at all, but it is still useful to the individual who initiated it. Study, then, is often contemplative in nature (Canadian Senior Dictionary, 1979). Although, experience, by comparison, is practical in nature. Explanation for learning, can cast in different ways. for example, there is no meaning in a given situation until we relate our own experiences to it (Jarvis, 1987).

LEARNING AND EDUCATION

For decades, educational psychologists have studied the learning process. They concluded that learning is equated to a change in behavior. Beyond this important conviction, very little consensus about what characterizes the learning process exists and there is no common understanding (Hansen, 2000). Furthermore they (Psychologists) have shown that knowledge can be acquired independent of practical action, by observing and imitating others and by extracting knowledge from experiences coded in text (Buchmann & Schwille, 1983). Everyone can think and solve problems, but it is obvious that there are wide differences in this ability among individuals at all age levels (Klausmier, 1971). Although experiential, or experience-based learning can be regarded as the earliest approach to learning for the human race, the significance and potential of it has not been fully recognized yet. In the formal education system it has tended to be developed and regarded as somehow fundamentally inferior to those organized forms of knowledge which have been constructed as subjects or disciplines. The practical and the applied do not tend to have the same status in educational institutions as the academic and the abstract. Besides this, the role of a teacher in the learning process has been enumerated by Rogers (1951). He believes no one learns anything of significance from someone else. Instead, learning takes place when a learner is intrinsically motivated to learn and undertakes to learn something on his/her own. Infact Scholars from Finland attempted to describe how teachers perceive the learning process. What happens in schools, in their opinion, can best be described as "study." They (scholars) done a comparative analysis which helps show how study and learning are related. In their analysis they define study as what students do in response to teacher initiatives. On the other hand (Kansanen, et al., 1997) described learning as the interaction, course, program, or other experience in which learning takes place, whether it occurs in traditional academic settings (schools, classrooms) or non-traditional settings (outside-of-school locations, outdoor environments), or whether it includes traditional educational interactions (students learning from teachers and professors) or nontraditional interactions (students learning through games and interactive software applications). Meanwhile (UNESCO, 2005) estimated globally, the growth in the demand for learning has already outstripped the ability of traditional education to supply it—and this is only the beginning. Apart from this (Thomas, 1990) provided an example, if learning is such an elusive concept to define, why not try to analyze what it means by comparing it to other known concepts. In this instance a comparison of what it means "to study" versus "to experience" might reveal what learning is thought to be. Could such an analysis reveal the real essence of learning? What does it mean to experience something as opposed to study it? What is the relationship of these two distinct actions and how do they impact on learning? Besides this, the difficult time some students have with their learning in general often has to do with how they perceive themselves in relation to that learning (Purkey, 1970). Answers to these queries will help us to develop higher levels of education which lead to greater schooling for the next generation, improved child health, lower crime rates, higher social cohesion, informed consumers, and informed political and democratic choices (Wolfe and Haveman , 2002).

TECHNOLOGY DRIVEN LEARNING

The goal is to improve users learning experiences to prepare them to enter a workforce that is not geographically constrained and expects them to have highly developed online collaboration skills. The pursuit of such benefits drives academics to incorporate new technological approaches in their teaching methodology

(Goode and Caicedo, 2010). Also due to constant demands to improve the quality of higher education within an increasingly digital world, technology is often seen as a way to increase learning and collaboration on campuses. The current generation of college students has grown up with technology, and these students are among the earliest adopters of new advances in technology (Jones, 2002; McHaney, 2011). Allowing students to connect to their campus community, collaborate with peers, acquire new information, and demonstrate their learning through technology is essential for college campuses seeking to meet the needs of today's college students. Though access and use of technology is highest in traditional age college students, disparity still exists in who uses technology and at what age they are exposed to it (Jones et al., 2009; Pew Research Center, 2012; Wilson, Wallin, & Reiser, 2003). Although traditional pedagogy tends to assume the acquisition of knowledge and understanding by the mind is a passive exercise. Psychological research and theory perpetuates this tradition by dividing the person into body and mind, into active and passive processes. Insufficient attention is paid to combinations of these categories. The result is a gap between what experience tells us about how we learn and what the experts tell us. Thought and action tend to have been separated, thinking and understanding to have been seen as abstract and general, therefore as teachable in abstract isolation from practical experience. In contrast, practical competence has often been spoken of as though it were just a matter of doing; skill is then taken to mean a combination of thoughtless behaviour habits, inculcatable through simple practice (Tomlinson & Kilner, 1992). Besides this, Social media tools are rapidly changing the communications landscape. Their emergence has impacted significantly how students learn and the way instructors teach. Today higher education settings, instructors, students, and others collaborate on the tasks of knowledge construction (Grover and Steward,2010). Thus these (social media tools) can have direct influence on the schooling. As it is positively associated with the diffusion of new technologies throughout society (Nelson. and Phelps, 1966).

NEED TO IMPROVE USER EXPERIENCES

Academic libraries are a valuable component within the framework of higher education. although they no longer serve the same purpose as in past decades academic libraries have continued to grow in a changing landscape while still remaining valuable partners in meeting the needs of students. Academic libraries have been able to maintain their relevance through the continuation and evolution of services offered. Today's users are incredibly complex. Their information-seeking behaviors have changed, and their engagement with and perception of our services are vastly different. Modern librarians must grapple daily with questions of how best to implement innovative new services, while also maintaining and updating the old in the digital age. By adopting user experience research techniques (by which we chiefly mean ethnography, usability, and service design) we can uncover the sort of users our libraries have today: users who do things in ways that we do not understand, that we find frustrating, or even condemn. The crucial point is that we are not our users, and just because they carry out tasks in a way that is alien to us does not mean that their way is wrong or broken. Instead, we need to see their approach as an opportunity to learn and discover. A user choosing to sit and photograph a 300-page reference book with a smartphone, thereby effectively creating their own unwieldy e-book, might seem ludicrous to us when they alternatively could sit and read it in the library or photocopy it (within legal limits, naturally). However, it is a scenario that bears some analysis and would reveal significant issues around convenience and preferred study environments were follow-up explorations to take place (NSS, 2015). Meanwhile US blog began talking about user experience of libraries as far back as 2007 and is still going strong today (http://dbl.lishost.org/blog/#.Vfso6m-zbIU). Here, Aaron Schmidt together with Amanda Etches (2014), wrote the highly practical and thought provoking Useful, Usable, Desirable about library user experience of spaces for many years. Their questions specifically encourage to ask ourselves about our library touch points, should be required reading for librarians everywhere. Besides this, Learning Management Systems (LMS) provide tools that can be used to manage teaching and learning activities and to integrate learning services in order to facilitate the procedures of both teaching and learning. The tools provided by LMS usually include: course-management tools for handling the provision of course content; tools for the management of online groups; communication aids; tools for collecting assignments; virtual classrooms; and tools that allow for learner assessments and course evaluations (Albarrak, Aboalsamh and Abouzahra, 2010). This can lead to E-learning. Which can be defined as the process of learning through the use of software and via electronic media, such as the Internet, satellite broadcasts, and traditional computer-supported learning (De Villiers, 2007).When using an E-learning application, the end user can have a positive experience; this can, in turn, be good for the business of the company that is presenting that application. According to (Griesemer, 2014). There can be numerous technologies which can be employed for changing the way instructors teach and students learn which includes • Weblogs. Weblogs or blogs, as they are known, are easily created and updateable websites that allow authors to publish to the Internet instantly, thus allowing instructors and students to communicate easily.

Wikis : A wiki is a collaborative web space where anyone can add or edit content that has already been published.

Really simple syndication (RSS) : RSS allows users to subscribe to news feeds originating either from blogs or more traditional web spaces like newspapers and magazines. The content comes to the reader instead of the reader having to retrieve the content.

Social bookmarking : Bookmarking sites allow users to

save and archive entire web pages. This enables users to produce a searchable, personalized Internet.

Online photograph galleries (OPG) : OPGs allow the posting of photographs that support sharing of ideas and experiences.

Audio/video casting (AVC) : AVC makes it easy to produce digital voice and video files and publish and distribute them over the Internet. It also supports basic, live-streaming television online.

Twitter : Twitter is a powerful tool for connecting with others and sharing content easily.

Social networking sites (SNS) : In addition to supporting wide area communication in both audio and video formats, SNSs help teach the network literacy that is required to navigate these new connections (Richardson, 2010)

CONCLUSION

In this time of rapid growth in information needs and in communication and digital technologies, academic libraries face a hard task, namely to provide effective and efficient ways of delivering information service to their users. Google and Amazon.com's customer gratification Web-based services have dramatically altered the information landscape, and now academic library users expect similar ease of use and immediate results when accessing information through the library gateway. In addition to this these libraries also face constant changes in subscription packages, formats, and technological advancements. The changing information landscape and users' demand force academic libraries to confront some tough questions. Walter and Marks (1981) suggested that, qualitatively speaking, half of an individual's reality resides in action. From a systems perspective, making experience a central element in school curriculum would mean that writing curriculum would change dramatically. On the other hand, interests outside of and inside the schooling infrastructure are calling for greater relevance in the curriculum and an experiential curriculum could be the answer. Although the motivation for the development of a learning society has involved creating more flexible institutions and finding ways to solve complex problems collectively. But that vision should be transplanted with broad spectrum of ideas. We need to understand how our physical environments, media, organizational structures, jobs, consumption habits, and relationships all nurture and frustrate the learning that matters to us as individuals and as communities. Whose learning counts, What are we learning for, How is experiences will be obtained in the most useful manner in the way of what we value.

REFERENCES

Albarrak, A.I., Aboalsamh, H.A., Abouzahra, M. (2010): Evaluating learning management systemsfor university medical education. In: IEEE International Conference on Education and Management Technology Retrieved from *www.formatex.info/ict/book/147-153.pdf*

Appleton, L. (2010). Living through super-convergence: Creating library and student support at Liverpool John Moores University. SCONUL Focus, 49, 67–70. Retrieved from www.educause.edu /space-strategies-new-learning-landscape

Aynsley-Smith, S. 2002. Widening participation and student support, Learning and Teaching in Action. Retrieved from www.celt.mmu.ac.uk/ltia/issue1/student_support.shtml

Baty, P. 2007. Open plan risk to collegiality. Times Higher Education Supplement. Retrieved from www.timeshighereducation.co.uk/story.asp?storyCode=208231&sectioncode=26

Canadian senior dictionary Retrieved from https://archive.org/stream/ERIC_EJ604485/ERIC_EJ604485_djvu.txt

De Villiers, M. (2007).: An action research approach to the design, development and evaluation of an interactive e-learning tutorial in a cognitive domain. J. Inf. Technol. Educ. 6, 455–479 Retrieved from https://eric.ed.gov/?id=EJ807683

Education and Learning in Wales.(2002). Space Management: A Good Practice Guide. Retrieved from www.smg.ac.uk/documents/swanspace.pdf

Jarvis, P. (1987). Meaningful and Meaningless Experience: Towards an Analysis of Learning from Life. Adult Education Quarterly, 37, 164-172. Retrieved from Journals.sagepub.com/doi/abs/10.1177/0001848187037003004

Griesemer - Quality Approaches in Higher 8 Education Vol. 3, No. 1 Retrieved from asq.org/edu/2014/.../using-social-media-to-enhance-students-learning-experiences.pdf

Gange,(1970). Retrieved from www.aect.org/edtech/ed1/18/18-03.html

Grover and Steward (2010). Defining Interactive Social Media in an Educational Context, Cutting-Edge Social Media Approaches to Business Education, Information Age. Retrieved from www.grover.../Unit%26%20y%20Guide%20Answers5.html

Goode and Caicedo (2010) Social Media Overload: What Works Best? Cutting-Edge Social Media Retrieved from www.aect.org/edtech/ed1/18/18-03.html

Mayers(1993). Retrieved from *www.mayfieldschools.org/.../Unit%206%20Study%20Guide%20Answers5.pdf*

Nelson, R. and Phelps, E. (1966) Investment in Humans, Technological Diffusion, and Economic Growth. American Economic Review. 56(2), pp.69-70. Retrieved from federation.ens.fr/wheberg/parischoeco/formation/fcses/_.../0607s1_lect02_a.pdf

NSS, 2015. The National Student Survey. Retrieved from www.thestudentsurvey.com

Kolb, D. A. (1984). Experiential learning: Experience as the source of learning and development. Englewood Cliffs: Prentice Hall. Retrieved from https://academic.regis.edu/ed205/kolb.pdf

Lewin, K. (1951). Field theory in social science. New York: Harper & Row. Retrieved from www.sciepub.com/reference/377

Rogers, C. (1951). Client-centered therapy: Its current practice, implications and theory. Boston: Houghton Mifflin. Retrieved from https://www.goodreads.com/book/show/1181940.Client_Centered_Therapy (Richardson,W. ,2010) .Blogs, Wikis, Podcasts, and Other Powerful Web Tools for Classrooms. SAGE Retrieved from https://books.google.co.in/books?hl=en&lr=&id=1L9q4LUvmiAC&oi=fnd&pg=PR1&dq=(Richardson,+2010)+social+tools+ can+be+employed+for+changing +the+way+instructors +teach+and+ students+learn&ots=Q5SeFpHZgt &sig=uaamSDfzyqX_azLVkN2UopckCIU#v=onepage&q&f=false

(UNESCO,2005). *Towards knowledge societies - UNESDOC Database - Unesco* Retrieved from unesdoc.unesco.org/images/0014/001418/141843e.pdf

Wolfe, B. and Haveman, R. (2002) Social and nonmarket benefits from education in an advanced economy Retrieved from citeseerx.ist.psu.edu/viewdoc/download?doi=10.1.1.196.8186&rep=rep1

Webester Retrieved from https://www.merriam-webster.com/dictionary/provided

14

Revisiting Information Science : Theoretical, Practical and Philosophical Approches

Guptnath Trivedi
Junior Research Fellow, Department of Library and Information Science
Banaras Hindu University, Varanasi-221005

ABSTRACT

The present study is the exploration of the concept "Information Science" from three different dimensions viz. theoretical, practical and philosophical dimensions. The definitions here provided have great authoritative values. It is an attempt to revisit the very popular concept which are discussed in terms of discipline, professional field of practice and its interconnection with philosophy. The meaning of "Science" part in information science has been discussed and also nature and characteristics of Information science has been discussed in this paper. The overall conclusion points have been drawn regarding the concept which will help to create and develop a basic idea about Information science.

Keywords : Information Science, Documentation, Philosophy, Librarianship.

INTRODUCTION

While stating Information science, Claude Shannon once said "It is hardly to be expected that a single concept of information would satisfactory account for the numerous possible applications of this general field" (Shannon,1948). This conceptualized that the term Information can have different meanings and perspective to understand and define, and therefore the "science of information"(Information Science) can also have a broad scope of study. Since last 5 decades the term Information Science has been defined by various professionals and philosophers representing library and information science, information communication and data flow technology, measuring information and its degree of informativeness and various allied disciplines, and there are abundant literature available in recorded form which questioned the term "Information Science" for exhibiting multi- dimensional characteristics . The dual anomalies of defining Information Science as a discipline or a subject of Professional practice creates need to define the term from different perspective from time to time and also because the dynamic and trendy nature of Information field. The present study is slanted towards understanding the philosophy and theory of information science and also it's practices among information professionals ie, how they use this concept in the creation of knowledge as output or any other form of organizational competency.

DEFINING INFORMATION SCIENCE

Various definitions that established and elicited worldwide attention while defining the term information science are discussed below:

1. While synthesizing the three basic ideas proposed by Robert S. Taylor (Taylor, Robert S., 1966 in Annual review of science and technology), H. Borko (1968) defined "Information science is that discipline that investigates the property and behavior of information, the forces governing the flow of information and the means of processing information

for optimum accessibility and usability. It is concerned with that body of knowledge relating to origination, collection, organization, storage, retrieval, interpretation, transmission, transformation and utilization of information" (Borko, H., 1968).

2. "Information Scienceis, or should be, involved with the whole concept of knowledge in whatever form its manifestations may take" (Shera,Jesse.,1973).
3. "Information science brings together and uses the theories, principles, techniques and technologies of a varieties of disciplines towards the solution of Information problems" (William, M.E., 1987/88)
4. "The concept has different meanings, which imply different knowledge domain. Different knowledge domains imply different fields. Nevertheless, all of them are represented by the same name, information science. No wonders that scholars, Practitioners and students are confused" (Zins,Chaim.,2007)
5. T. Saracevic provided a general idea about the nature of Information Science while stating as: "Information Science is the science and pratice dealing with the effective collection, storage, retrieval and use of information. It is concerned with recorded information and knowledge, and the technologies and related services that facilitates their management and use" (Saracevic, 2009)
6. T.D. Wilson at University of Sheffield, UK , defined "Information Science is that set of practices and related disciplinary studies which is concerned with the generation, transmission, organization, storage, retrieval and use of information together with the studies of the user of information"
7. Anthony Debons at University of Pittsburgh, USA defined "Information Science is that area of study and practice which attempts to determine the laws and principles

pertaining to the analysis, design and evaluation of data, information and knowledge system"

8. Prof. Michael Buckland, at University of California, Berkeley states as "Information science which is formerly known as Documentation simply concerned with the creation, dissemination and utilization of knowledge"

THE "SCIENCE" OF INFORMATION

While answering about science part of Information Prof. Buckland(2012) states three basic subjective basis as;

(a) Science part of Information is related with science part of computer (deals with computing, IT, and algorithms)

(b) Science part of Information is related with entropy and other related phenomena like Information Physics

(c) Science part of Information deals with recorded Information in documents and hard drives with their clear semantics and analytics.

In short there can be a general perspective, (although there may be different opinion) that science part in Information science is basically the analytical and quantitative part that mainly deals with the measurement of Information and it's scholarly communication. Informatics and Scientometrics deals with the same concept and that is why these are credited among one of the highest enriched field as per as research is concerned. The phenomena of Information forecasting also supports science part of Information science as it provides a means of anticipating future message needs of a society or predicting the necessary types of Information that will allow smooth social functioning (Hanneman,1972).

NATURE AND CHARACTERISTICS OF INFORMATION SCIENCE

From the above mentioned concepts it can be clearly said that Information Science exhibit dual nature ie, it can be seen from academic discipline point of view and at the same time as a field of professional practice. Although Paul Hirst a great known philosopher mentioned that a field of study mainly comprises a topic or a subject of interest, using any of the form of knowledge-Philosophical, Sociological etc. Thus the nature of Information Science can be noticed in a generalized definition of Information Science as-

> "a multidisciplinary field of study, that involve different form of knowledge, coherenced by focusing on central concept of human recorded information" (Robinson and bawden, 2012).

Characteristics of Information Science can be viewed with binomial concepts

(a) Information Science as a discipline : Includes four basic features of Information Science viz.

- Multidisciplinary in nature (includes inter-study of various disciplines like linguistics, communication theory, Cognitive Science, Librarianship and archival science, Computer science, Mathematics, Education etc.)
- Based on strong glinths of Information Technology, as IT has been a driving force for the elevation and development of Information science as a discipline,
- Acts as a participant like others disciplines in the creation of Information society and cultural coherence.
- Manages decisions, policies infrastructure to increase organizational competencies.

(b) Information Science as a field of professional practice : The science of Information that Deals with the practical point of view or used for professional accomplishment through documentation or other media of explicit knowledge representation. The process mainly consists of collection, organization, Storage, Retrieval, Dissemination, and Use of Information.

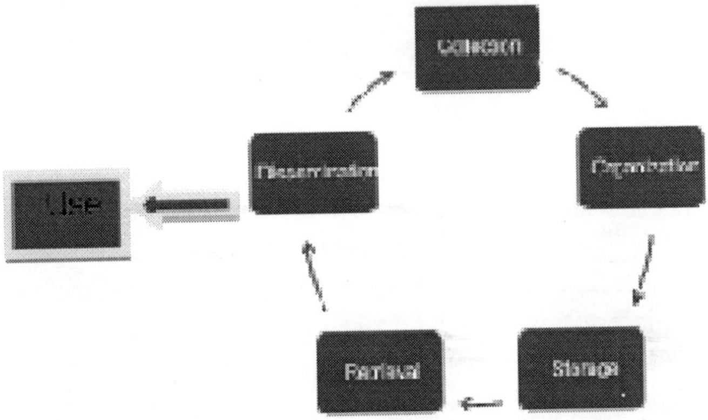

PHILOSOPHICAL ASPECT OF INFORMATION SCIENCE

Both Philosophy and Information Science have great relevance on one another. while information science has a broad disciplinary coverage in which we study the phenomena like information processing, dissemination and theory of information from its social, technical and economic view points, the philosophy deals with the Four fundamental components that surrounds the concepts of Information and Knowledge in a great sense.

The four basic components are as follows-

Epistemology : The branch of philosophy that deals with the study of theory of knowledge, how knowledge creates, different classifications of knowledge, how anyone know about anything, the strong concept and surety behind our knowing and knowledge etc.

Metaphysics : The branch of philosophy that deals with

the study of existence of anything, what sort of things can exist etc. This branch has a depth classification in terms of representation and organization of knowledge and information. the three sub- categories that can be studied for these concepts are: (1) Cosmology (2) Cosmogony and (3) Ontology. Ontology and its related phenomena are now a days has been an important field of research and study among libraries and information professionals, which basically deals with the classification and representation of knowledge and information on the Web. many web languages like OWL (Ontological Web Language) are arise for schematic web representation of information and knowledge.

Logic : The branch deals with study of reasons and causes with the help of intellect and persuasion. These are of two types- (1) Deductive logic and (2) Inductive logic. while deductive logic based on certain premises and bounds to be true if premises are true for any information, the inductive logic is different in the sense that it does not based on premises.

Ethics : The branch of philosophy that deals with the study of human behavior, their actions and conduct, it also deals with the explanation of someone being right or true in his/her conduct or actions.

Apart from these basic concepts, many philosophers have discussed this topic which is directly beneficial for information science. Floridi, Dretske, and Popper are those ones whom background is philosophy but has a great relevance with Information science and related issues. Michael Buckland, Briger Hjorland and Marcia J. Bates , Jesse Shera are those among disciplinary scholars in information science but known as for their philosophical contribution to Information Science.

CONCLUSIONS

we can conclude with the following assumptions that may include further study and exploration about the same topic.

- Information Science is a multi-disciplinary field of study and it's really difficult to find its actual boundary and breadth as it grown from traditional concepts of librarianship and documentation but has a strong interlinking with Computer science and IT.

- It is also a field of practical practice in which we deals with recorded information and its further processing and usability.
- There are many approaches and basis for defining Information Science from different perspectives.
- There is no any universally acceptable philosophical background of Information science. Different philosophers and Information Scientists defines it from their own perspective.
- There is a great possibility for further studies in theoretical and philosophical aspects of Information Science.

REFERENCES

1. Borko, H. (1968) Information science : what is it?, *Journal of the American Society for Information Science,* 19(1), 3-5.
2. Shera, J. (1973) and Cleveland, D.B. (1977) History and foundation of information science, *Annual Review of Information Science and technology*, 12, 249-75.
3. Farradane, J. (1976) Towards a true information science, *The Information Scientists*, 10(3), 91-101.
4. Ingwersen, P.(1992) Information and information science in context, *Libri,* 42(2), 99-135.
5. Buckland, M.K. and Liu, Z. (1995) History of information science, *Annual Review of Information Science and Technology,*30, 385-416.
6. Hjorland, B. (2000) Library and information science : practice, theory and philosophical basis, *Information Processing and Management*, 36(3), 504-31.
7. Buckland, M.K.(1996) Documentation, Information science and library science in the USA, *Information Processing and Management*, 32(1), 63-76.
8. Bates, M.J. (1996) The invisible substrate of information science, *Journal of the American Society for Information Science,* 50(12), 1043-50
9. Floridi, L. (2002) On defining library and information science as applies

philosophy of information, *Social Epistemology,* 16(1), 37-49.

10. Bates, M.J. (2007) Defining the information discipline in encyclopedia development, *Information Research*, 12(4), [online] available at http://information.net/ir/12-4/colis29.html.

11. Bawden, D. (2007) Information seeking and information retrival: the core of the information curriculum, *Journal of Education for Library and Information Science*, 48(2), 125-38.

12. Wilson, T.D. (2010) Information and information science : an address on the occasion of recieving the award of Doctor Honoris Causa, at the University of Murcia, September 2010, *Information Research,* 15(4), paper 439 [online] available at http://InformationR.net/ir/15-4/paper439.html.

13. Buckland, M.K.(2012) What kind of science can information science be?, *Journal of the American Society for Information Science,* 63(1), 1-7.

14. Bawden, D. and Robinson, Lyn (2012) *Introduction to information science*, London : Facet.

15

Scientometrics as A Research Evaluation Tool: A Conceptual Approach

Sanjay Kumar Maurya
Research Scholar, Department of Library & Information Science
Mizoram University, Aizawl – 796 004

ABSTRACT

Paper deals with the conceptual background of scientometrics. Paper relates scientometrics with bibliometrics, informetrics, librametrics, and altmetrics. Various scientometrics indicators like impact factor, h-index, g-index, Eigenfactor, immediacy index, and SNIP have been discussed alongwith various scientometric tools.

Keywords : Scientometrics, Research Assessment, Scientometric Indicators, Mapping, Visualization.

CONCEPT OF SCIENTOMETRICS

Library and Information Science (LIS) has witnessed several quantitative and qualitative methods for evaluating research at both macro and micro level over the last few decades. "Scientometric research is the quantitative mathematical study of science and technology, encompassing both bibliometric and economic analysis is expanding at an enormous pace".[1] At present different tools like Librametrics, Bibliometrics, Scientometrics, Informetrics, Webometrics and Altmetrics are used for analyzing information communication. "The term scientometrics has been first used as a translation of the Russian term "naukometriya" (measurement of science) coined by Nalimov and Mulchenko in 1969" (Zhao & Zhao, 2014). Scientometrics was first defined by Nalimov "as developing the quantitative methods of the research on the development of science as an informational process" (Mingers & Leydesdorff, 2015). Hess in 1997 defined scientometrics as the "quantitative study of science, communication in science, and science policy. Scientometric field has evolved over time from the study of indices for improving information retrieval from peer-reviewed scientific publications to cover other types of documents and information sources relating to science and technology".[2] According to Pouris, "scientometrics is for science what econometrics is for economics. Therefore, it is application of quantitative techniques (systems analysis, mathematical and statistical techniques etc.) to scientific communication (science output, science policy, science administration etc.)."[3] According to Tague-Sutcliffe, scientometrics is "the study of the quantitative aspects of science as a discipline or economic activity."[4]

At present, multidimensional research changed the scenario, as a result exponential growth of literature and different evolutionary studies about the effectiveness and efficiency of literature began with help of scientometric studies. "Scientometric studies throw light on the pattern of growth of literature, collaborative research, ranking of journals, inter-relationship among different branches of knowledge, productivity and influence of authors, pattern of collection built up, and their uses etc. It is the need of the time to understand the characteristics of literature such as growth and scatter, collaborative research trends, highly productive journals, research productivity of institutes, utilization and consumption in planning and designing of information systems are useful in developing need based collection of resources, proper planning of library services and also useful in solving some of the problems of the library and research organization by taking prompt decision."[5] The broader and thematic possibility of scientometrics study includes issues such as "quantitative studies of scientists, projects, funding of research, research infrastructure, etc.; quantitative studies of publications, patents, and citations by institutions, countries, languages, co-authorships, thematic fields, etc.; investigations and monitoring of individual, institutional, or state research production; identification of relations between different research disciplines; studies of the internationalization of science; tracing the development of a given scientific field, research community, institution, etc.; revealing of emerging research problems; assessing the impact factor of scientific journals; The main set of research instruments, applied in scientometrics, comprises observation, measuring, mathematical processing, comparison, classification, generalization, visualization, and interpretation of data."[6]

INDICATORS OF SCIENTOMETRICS

Scientometrics indicators used in monitoring the evolution of research, generally common indexes of scientometrics are calculated mainly in four variables i.e. author, publication, reference and citation. Citation is the most valid and core index of scientometrics and rest of indexes have been formed or created to adjust or improve the citation. Some of the most important scientometrics indexes are described as follows:

(a) Impact Factor (IF)

"The impact factor (IF) is frequently used as an indicator of the importance of a journal to its field. It was first introduced by Eugene Garfield, the founder of the Institute for Scientific Information. Although IF is widely used by institutions and clinicians, people have widespread mis-conception regarding the method for calculating the Journal IF (JIF), its significance and how it can be utilized. The IF of a journal is not associated to the factors like quality of peer review process and quality of content of the journal, but is a measure that reflects the average number of citations to articles published in journals, books, thesis, project reports, newspapers, conference/seminar proceedings, documents published in Internet, notes, and any other approved documents. Impact factor can be calculated after completing the minimum of 3 years of publication; for that reason journal IF cannot be calculated for new journals. The journal with the highest IF is the one that published the most commonly cited articles over a 2-year period. The IF applies only to journals, not to individual articles or individual scientists unlike the "H-index." The relative number of citations an individual article receives is better evaluated as "citation impact." In a given year, the IF of a journal is the average number of citations received per article published in that journal during the two preceding years. IFs are calculated each year by Thomson Scientific for those journals that it indexes, and are published in Journal Citation Reports. For example if a journal has an IF of 3 in 2008, then its papers published in 2006 and 2007 received three citations each on average in 2008. The 2008 IFs are actually published in 2009; they cannot be calculated until all of the 2008 publications have been processed by the indexing agency (Thomson Reuters). The IF of any journal may be calculated by the formula:

2012 impact factor =A/B

Where A is the number of times articles published in 2010 and 2011 were cited by indexed journals during 2012. B is the total number of citable items like articles and reviews published by that journal in 2010 and 2011." (Sharma, Sarin, Gupta, Sachdeva & Desai, 2014).

(b) Immediacy Index

"The Immediacy Index is the average number of times an article is cited in the year it is published. The Immediacy Index is calculated by dividing the number of citations to articles published in a given year by the number of articles published in that year. Because it is a per-article average, the Immediacy Index tends to discount the advantage of large journals over small ones. However, frequently issued journals may have an advantage because an article published early in the year has a better chance of being cited than one published later in the year. Many publications that publish late in the year have chance of low Immediacy Index. For comparing journals specializing in cutting-edge research, the Immediacy Index can provide a useful perspective."[7]

(c) h-index

The h-index is short for the Hirsch index, which was introduced by Jorge E. Hirsch (2005) as a way to quantify the productivity and impact of an individual author. Similar to how the IF is now be used to measure a journal or an author to their scientific field, the *h*-index has become another measure of relative impact of scientific publications. While the IF is derived from the quotient of total citations and total papers in a two-year span, the *h*-index is simply a count of the largest number of papers (h) from a journal or author that have at least (h) number of citations (Noruzi, 2016).

(d) g-index

The g-index was first suggested by Leo Egghe in 2006. Like *h*-index it is also author level metrics to analyze scientific productivity. "G-index is calculated based on the distribution of citations received by a given researcher's publications, such that given a set of articles ranked in decreasing order of the number of citations that they received, the g-index is the unique largest number such that the top *g* articles received together at least g^2 citations. It can be equivalently defined as the largest number *n* of highly cited articles for which the average number of citations is at least *n*."[8]

(e) SNIP

Source Normalized Impact per Paper (SNIP) measures

contextual citation impact by weighting citations based on the total number of citations in a subject field. The impact of a single citation is given higher value in subject areas where citations are less likely, and vice-versa. Unlike the well-known journal impact factor, SNIP corrects for differences in citation practices between scientific fields, thereby allowing for more accurate between-field comparisons of citation impact. The source normalized impact per publication, calculated as the number of citations given in the present year to publications in the past three years divided by the total number of publications in the past three years.[9]

(f) Eigenfactor

The Eigenfactor came out of the Metrics Eigenfactor Project in 2008, a bibliometric research project conducted by Professor Carl Bergstrom and his laboratory at University of Washington. The Eigenfactor Score measures the number of times articles from the journal published in the past five years has been cited in the Journal Citation Reports (JCR) year. Like the Impact Factor, the Eigenfactor Score is essentially a ratio of number of citations to total number of articles. However, unlike the Impact Factor, the Eigenfactor Score:

- Counts citations to journals in both the sciences and social sciences.
- Eliminates self-citations. Every reference from one article in a journal to another article from the same journal is discounted.
- Weights each reference according to a stochastic measure of the amount of time researchers spend reading the journal.

Eigenfactor scores are scaled so that the sum of the Eigenfactor scores of all journals listed in Thomson's Journal Citation Reports (JCR) is 100. The Eigenfactor uses Thomson Reuters Web of Science citation data" (Tchangalova, n.d.).

SCIENTOMETRIC ANALYSIS, MAPPING AND VISUALIZATION SOFTWARE

As per definition of Online Dictionary of Library and Information Science (ODLIS) scientometric software is "a set of computer based programs, designed and developed to analyze citation based bibliographic data as input to perform the specific tasks i.e. structural analysis of scholarly communication, mapping of scientific research, creation of metrics based social maps, information representation and organisation, visualization of research, micro level analysis (co-word, co-author, cited references, bibliographic coupling, co-citation) etc. as output. Scientometric analysis, mapping and visualization software facilitates its users to draw the maps for visual representation of scientific research based on citation data, to study the structural, temporal and dynamics of a subject discipline. Most of these software are based on the modern algorithms, mathematical and statistical methods, graphs theory, network science, etc." (Kumar, Shivarama & Choukimath, 2015). Some of the related softwares are described below:

(a) BibExcel

It is free software for academic and non-profit use. It is developed by Olle Persson of Sweden. Its popularity lies in the fact that it can do most type of commonly done bibliometric analysis. Frequency distribution (Authors, Titles, Citations, or any field specified), and Co-occurrence analysis (includes Co-citation analysis, Bibliographic coupling, Co-author analysis, Co-word analysis) are the most widely used functionalities in BibExcel. One unique feature of the tool is it uses two counting methods – Whole Counts and Fractional Counts. The distinction between the two is not difficult to understand. For example, for a three-authored article, while the whole count method assigns one count for each author; the fractional count method assigns one third of the count for each author. Both these counting methods are in vogue in bibliometrics. A useful feature in Bibexcel is the one that enables us to produce data matrices for export to statistical software. It allows easy interaction with other software, e.g. Pajek, Excel, SPSS, etc. The program offers the user high degree of flexibility in both data management and analysis and this flexibility is one of the program's real strengths. It is, for example, possible to use other data sources than Web of Science, and Bibexcel can in fact deal with data other than bibliographic records."[10]

(b) CiteSpace

CiteSpace is a freely available Java application for visualizing and analyzing trends and patterns in scientific literature. It is designed as a tool for progressive knowledge domain visualization (Chen, 2004). It focuses on finding critical points in the development of a field or a domain, especially intellectual turning points and pivotal points. Detailed case studies are given in (Chen, 2006) and other publications. CiteSpace provides various functions to facilitate the understanding and interpretation of network patterns and historical patterns, including identifying the fast-growth topical areas, finding citation hotspots in the land of publications, decomposing a network into clusters, automatic labeling clusters with terms from citing articles, geospatial patterns of collaboration, and unique areas of international collaboration.

CiteSpace supports structural and temporal analyses of a variety of networks derived from scientific publications, including collaboration networks, author co-citation networks, and document co-citation networks. It also supports networks of hybrid node types such as terms, institutions, and countries, and hybrid link types such as co-citation, co-occurrence, and directed citing links. The primary source of input data for CiteSpace is the Web of Science. Search for a topic of interest and download the search results (including full records and references). CiteSpace will handle the data from there. CiteSpace also provides some simple interfaces for obtaining data from PubMed, arXiv, ADS, and NSF Award Abstracts. CiteSpace can be used to generate geographic map overlays viewable in Google Earth based on the locations of authors."[11]

(c) HistCite

HistCite is a flexible software solution to aid researchers in visualizing the results of literature searches in the Web of Science. It is easy, fast, and provides perspectives and information not available from the Web of Science. HistCite can create clear and informative data tables and graphs in an HTML format readable in a Web browser. HistCite also outputs data in tables and publication-quality graphs. HistCite is a software implementation of algorithmic historiography, and has been developed by Eugene Garfield, founder of the Institute for Scientific Information and the inventor of citation analysis."[12]

(d) SciMAT

SciMAT (Science Mapping Analysis software Tool) is an open source science mapping software tool which incorporates methods, algorithms, and measures for all the steps in science mapping workflow, from pre-processing to the visualization of the results. SciMAT allows the user to carry out studies based on several kinds of bibliometric networks. Different normalization and similarity measures can be used over the data. Several clustering algorithms can be chosen to cut up the data. In the visualization module, three representations (strategic diagrams, cluster networks, and evolution areas) are jointly used, which allows the user to better understand the results."[13]

(e) SCI²

The Science of Science (SCI²) tool is a modular toolset specifically designed for the study of science. It supports the temporal, geospatial, topical, and network analysis and visualization of scholarly datasets at the micro (individual), meso (local), and macro (global) levels.

(f) Network Workbench

This project will design, evaluate, and operate a unique distributed, shared resources environment for large-scale network analysis, modeling, and visualization, named Network Workbench (NWB). The envisioned data-code-computing resources environment will provide a one-stop online portal for researchers, educators, and practitioners interested in the study of biomedical, social and behavioral science, physics, and other networks. The NWB will support network science research across scientific boundaries. Users of the NWB will have online access to major network datasets or can upload their own networks. They will be able to perform network analysis with the most effective algorithms available. In addition, they will be able to generate, run, and validate network models to advance their understanding of the structure and dynamics of particular networks. NWB will provide advanced visualization tools to interactively explore and understand specific networks, as well as their interaction with other types of networks."[14]

CONCLUSION

Scientometrics is the study of qualitative and quantitative measurement and analysis of scientific literature & scientific policy. The paper deals with the concept of scientometrics along with its implications at different level as well as some of the scientometric indicators like Impact Factor, Immediacy Index, h-index, g-index, SNIP, Eigenfactor. Besides these, software tools like Bibexcel, CiteSpace, HistCite, SciMAT, Sci^2 and Network Workbench are also discussed. In recent years various scientometric tools and indicators were developed which shape and extend its scope for evaluation and ranking at institutional level, journal level and individual level. Further the impact, visibility and ranking of these levels are analyzing at national, regional and international level. At present in the competitive age, there is more demand of user friendly softwares and suitable and efficient indicators which would look up the scientific communication from different perspectives; apart from certain demerits, scientometric study will take the level of research at high.

REFERENCES

Kumar, A., Shivarama, J., & Choukimath, P. A. (2015). Popular Scientometric Analysis,

Mapping and Visualisation Softwares: An Overview (p. 14). Presented at the 10th International CALIBER-2015, HP University and IIAS, Shimla, Himachal Pradesh, India.

Mingers, J., & Leydesdorff, L. (2015). A review of theory and practice in scientometrics.

European Journal of Operational Research, 246(1), 1–19. https://doi.org/10.1016/j.ejor.2015.04.002

Noruzi, A. (2016). Impact Factor, h-index, i10-index and i20-index of Webology. Webology, 13(1), 4.

Sharma, M., Sarin, A., Gupta, P., Sachdeva, S., & Desai, A. V. (2014). Journal Impact Factor: Its Use, Significance and Limitations. World Journal of Nuclear Medicine, 13(2), 146. https://doi.org/10.4103/1450-1147.139151

Tchangalova, N. (n.d.). LibGuides: Bibliometrics and Altmetrics: Measuring the Impact of Knowledge: Eigenfactor. Retrieved May 29, 2018, from http://lib.guides.umd.edu/bibliometrics/eigenfactor

Zhao, Y., & Zhao, R. (2014). Evolution of the Development of Scientometrics (pp. 905–912). Presented at the in iConference 2014 Proceedings, iSchools. https://doi.org/10.9776/14310

WEB REFERENCES

1. https://www.researchtrends.com/issue1-september-2007/sciomentrics-from-past-to-present/
2. http://www.oecd.org/sti/inno/scientometrics.htm.
3. http://shodhganga.inflibnet.ac.in/bitstream/10603/96697/8/08_chapter%202.pdf
4. http://shodhganga.inflibnet.ac.in/bitstream/10603/96697/8/08_chapter%202.pdf
5. http://shodhganga.inflibnet.ac.in/bitstream/10603/21200/6/08_chapter%201.pdf
6. http://www.bharatcollege.in/PDFs/scientometry-.pdf

7. http://ipscience-help.thomsonreuters.com/incitesLiveJCR/glossaryAZgroup/g7/7751-TRS.html
8. https://en.wikipedia.org/wiki/G-index
9. http://lib.guides.umd.edu/bibliometrics/SNIP
10. http://epgp.inflibnet.ac.in/epgpdata/uploads/epgp_content/library_and_information_science/informetrics_&_scientometrics/data_sources_and_software_tools_for_bibliometric_studies/et/333_et_m2.pdf
11. http://cluster.cis.drexel.edu/~cchen/citespace/
12. https://rmimr.wordpress.com/2007/06/21/histcite%E2%84%A2-bibiliographic-analysis-and-visualization- software/
13. http://sci2s.ugr.es/scimat/description.html
14. http://nwb.cns.iu.edu/citation.html

16

An Overview of Subject Gateways Specially for Library & Information Science in India : Trends & Issues

Tumpa Saha

Ex Student , University of North Bengal,

Department of Library & Information Science, West Bengal, India

ABSTRACT

Libraries have been undergoing tremendous developments in the era of 21st century, adapting to the advent of information technology in the day to day working. Electronic, Digital Libraries have arrived. OPAC, CDROM databases, Electronic journals and Internet access exist in most Libraries. Libraries are no longer storehouses but are becoming gateways of relevant information. The role of Librarians have become challenging enough to expect the increasing demands of users and catering to specific information needs. Librarians are also showing sufficient interest in introducing advanced technologies and innovative services in their Libraries. The primary objective and functions of libraries have not changed due to computerization. Only, the tools and techniques to achieve these objectives with ease and accuracy have. In the present day the focus is on Electronic Information. Thus it is not only acquiring, sources of information but providing access to information and sharing also. With the Internet, WWW and Information explosion, identification and extraction of information resources is an essential function of all libraries and information centres. The Electronic information sources are rapidly growing and with a wide variety in form and content it takes a lot of time to get the required information. There is thus a need to organize and classify this wide spectrum of information. The Web is quickly becoming the world's fastest growing repository of data. People are increasingly going to the Internet before they go to the library. Subject gateways "doing for Internet information resources what librarians do for books". With this as background, the author has tried to find out that how subject gateways are becoming the very useful tool for library professionals as well as users for searching and retrieving the particular documents from a wide Varity of documents.

Keywords : Information Communication Technology, www, Internet, subject gateways.

INTRODUCTION

Learners and researchers have a potentially vast range of resources available to them through the Internet and associated technologies .But, as the Internet increases in size and complexity, so do the associated usability and navigational issues. A range of strategies has been used to manage online information and provide different searching protocols, navigational aids and maps. Nonetheless, information overload persists. This information overload problem is well recognized and a number of structured resources and environments attempt to address it, such as search engines, information gateways and portals, digital libraries and virtual learning environments. In reality, users may need to adopt more of a 'mix and match' strategy, selecting individual features from relevant sources to meet their specific needs. Traditionally, academicians and researchers have turned to librarians to assist in the organisation and, ultimately, the retrieval of information.

Since the beginning of scholarly activity libraries have organized information based upon the scholar's area of study. Subject collections comprised of materials in various formats have drawn scholars to the library. Today libraries organize myriad online resources to assist selected user communities, again based upon areas of study through the development of subject gateways or portals. However, a critical issue remains how best to broker access to heterogeneous information and learning resources. In this paper author have tried to decline a concise information about subject Gateway related to the field of LIS . here some multisubject gateways are asked for an effective result of this study.

SUBJECT GATEWAY

Subject gateways are a collection of websites on a particular subject. Unlike search engines (which find both good and poor quality websites randomly sorted) subject gateways contain only web resources that have been evaluated by subject specialists.

The Web is quickly becoming the world's fastest growing repository of data. People are increasingly going to the Internet before they go to the library. Subject gateways "doing for Internet information resources what librarians do for books". An Internet search tool to help people find information on the Internet e.g.: electronic journals software datasets electronic books mailing lists /discussion groups (and their archives) articles / papers. Subject Gateways are Internet services which support systematic discovery of high quality information provide links to resources accessible via the Internet, are based on resource descriptions provide browsing and searching access to the resources via a subject structure The key ingredient ...the semantics that only the human factor can bring: subject specialists library / information Professionals.

Features of Gateways

There are a considerable number of Web-based gateways that can be used to locate network-based resources in some particular subject area. Nearly all of these gateways have unique features, additional subject-based services, and different approaches to how information about network-based resources is stored in the resource description database.

Basic gateway facilities

Most subject gateways allow the end-user to either search or browse the database of resource descriptions.

Additional searching facilities

Some gateways provide extra facilities for enhanced searching.

Additional subject-related services

Some subject gateways have built a considerable number of related services and information sources around their core searchable/browsable gateway.

GATEWAYS SUBJECT WISE

Library and Information Science

- LIS Learning
- LISGateway.com
- Infolibrarian
- AILLMIS- All India Libraries and Librarians Management Information System

Multidisciplinary

- DMOZ
- INFOPORT: INFLIBNET Subject Gateway for Indian Electronic-Resources
- The WWW Virtual Library
- ipl2

All above subject gateways are discussed below along with their home page for a clear idea.

This contents covered in the ***LISGATEWAY.COM*** are purely to serve the academic community. The gateway links to various electronic resources available on the Internet, rather it organizes & catalogs the digital information available on web, pertaining to LIS.

LIS LEARNING is a humble initiative to bring together the all library and information science professionals in to one platform, so that they can enhance their knowledge and share their expertise and views. The portal envisages a space for teachers and other professionals to express their ideas on any subject that touches their professional lives, which also involves the uploading of material created by and for library professionals in English Language.

The portal *LIS Learning* will help to impart LIS education in all types of professionals, researchers and other learners. The whole information has been divided in to various categories such as Faculty Corner, Professionals Corner, Researchers Corner, Students Corner etc. to meet the information requirements of the all sections of the LIS community. Links will be provided to websites of other organizations, institutions and people to provide access for information professionals and library students.The project has been funded by University Grants Commission (UGC), New Delhi under its Major Research Project (2012-2014).

Infolibrarian embarked on its journey to provide useful information to Library and Information Science [LIS] professionals in 2000. Soon, within a span of a year or so, it received good response from fellow LIS professionals. The site also made it to the list of useful resources of United Nations, UNESCO, Subject Directories etc. Today, we realise the name 'infolibrarian' has become omnipresent among the professional circles in India and abroad. **We very much appreciate and sincerley thank you for your patronage** extended to us and we hope you will continue to support us in meeting our goals.

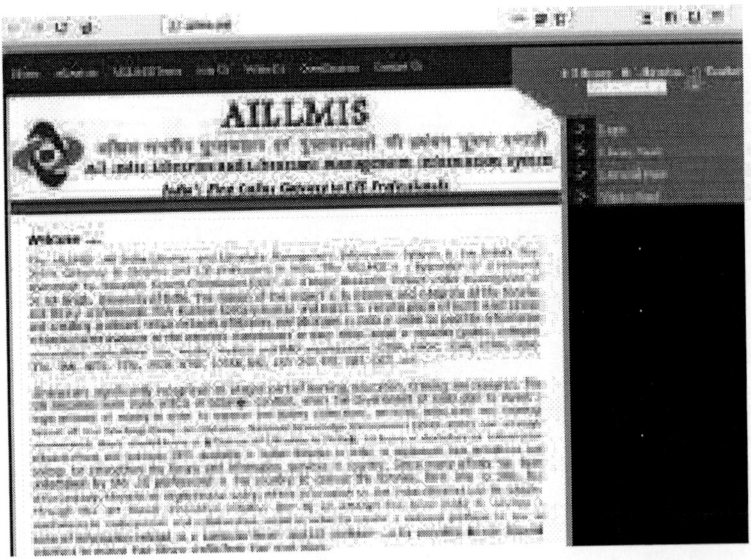

The ***AILLMIS***- All India Libraries and Librarians Management Information System is the India's First Online Gateway to Libraries and LIS professions in India. The AILLMIS is a by product of a research sponsored by University Grants Commission (UGC) as a Major Research Project under investigation of Dr. KP Singh, University of Delhi. The mission of the project is to interlink and integrate all the libraries and library professionals from Kashmir to Kanyakumari and Ketch to remote place of north east states and creating a vibrant virtual network of libraries and librarians in India in order to pool the information infrastructures available in the different stakeholders of each focus areas of libraries (public, colleges, universities, agriculture, law, media, medical and R&D organizations (CSIR, DRDO, ICAR, ICMR, ISRO, IITs, IIMs, NITs, IIITs, IISER, ICFRI, ICSSR, BSI, ASI, ZSI, FSI, DBT, DST, etc.).

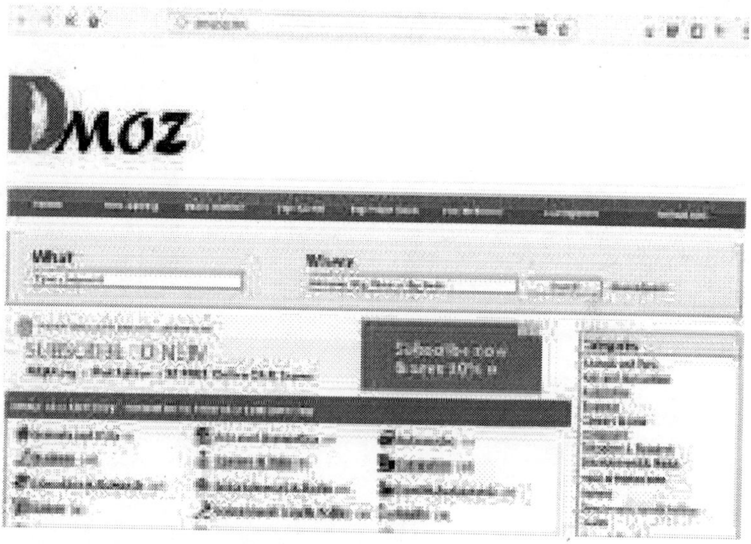

DMOZ (from *directory.mozilla.org*, an earlier *domain name*) was a multilingual *open-content directory* of *World Wide Web* links. The site and community who maintained it were also known as the Open Directory Project (ODP). It was owned by *AOL* (now a part of *Verizon*'s *Oath Inc.*) but constructed and maintained by a *community* of volunteer editors.DMOZ used a hierarchical *ontology* scheme for organizing site listings. Listings on a similar topic were grouped into categories which then included smaller categories.DMOZ closed on March 17, 2017 because AOL no longer wished to support the project. The website became a single landing page on that day, with links to a static archive of DMOZ, and to the DMOZ discussion forum, where plans to rebrand and relaunch the directory are being discussed.As of September 2017, a non-editable mirror remained available at dmoztools.net, and it was stated that while the DMOZ URL would not return, a successor version of the directory would, at Curlie.org.

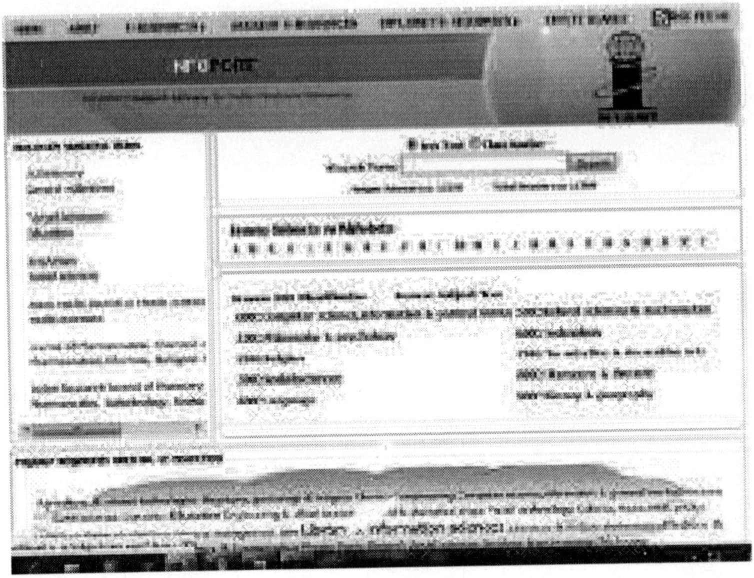

The INFLIBNET Centre promotes open access to Indian scholarly content through the ***InfoPort***: A Subject Gateway for Indian Electronic-Resources. While Centre uses and promotes Intute, a well-known subject gateway developed by MIMAS, UK, the InfoPort is designed and developed to serve as a comprehensive gateway to all Indian scholarly content. The gateway open-ups the Indian scholarly content scattered over the Internet through an integrated interface that support search, browse and multiple listing. The InfoPort selectively catalogues online resources of Indian origin on diversified subjects available in open access through an elaborate process of testing and evaluation. The Centre proposes to collaborate with librarians and scholars in college and universities in the process of identification and selection of resources.The universe of knowledge is divided into different subject groups. According to the Dewey Decimal Classification, the universe of knowledge is scattered from 000 to 999. InfoPort is classified according to DDC, indexed subjectwise and arranged alphabetically subjects.

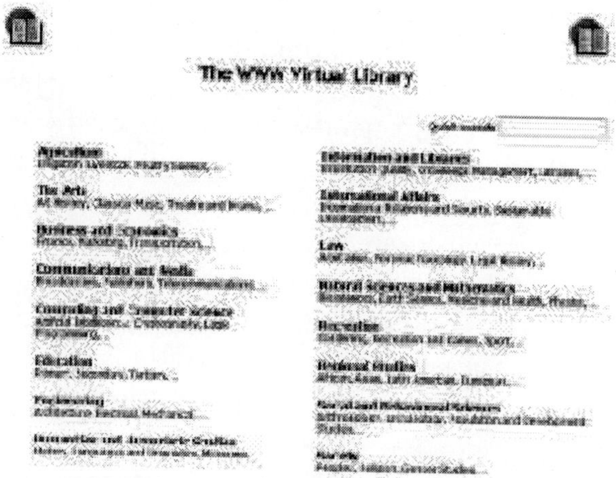

The ***WWW Virtual Library*** (VL) is *the oldest catalogue of the Web*, started by Tim Berners-Lee, the creator of HTML and of the Web itself, in 1991 at CERN in Geneva. Unlike commercial catalogues, it is run by a loose confederation of volunteers, who compile pages of key links for particular areas in which they are expert; even though it isn't the biggest index of the Web, the VL pages are widely recognised as being amongst the highest-quality guides to particular sections of the Web.

ipl2 is a public service organization and a learning/teaching environment. To date, thousands of students and volunteer library and information science professionals have been involved in answering reference questions for our Ask an ipl2 Librarian service and in designing, building, creating and maintaining the ipl2's collections. It is through the efforts of these students and volunteers that the ipl2 continues to thrive to this day.

In January 2010, the website "ipl2: information you can trust" was launched, merging the collections of resources from the Internet Public Library (IPL) and the Librarians' Internet Index (LII) websites. The site is hosted by *The College of Computing & Informatics at Drexel University*, and a *consortium of colleges and universities* with programs in information science are involved in developing and maintaining the ipl2.

WHY GATEWAY IS BETTER THAN THE SEARCH ENGINE

Using a subject gateway instead of a general search engine can result in the return of more genuine and relevant web pages from our search. If we do wish to use a search engine, then we will have to think more carefully about appraising the information we retrieve from the web before we can rely on it as a basis for our study or research. Subject gateways are portals to web pages in a particular subject area. They usually provide a search interface which allows us to find relevant web pages. An added advantage is that they usually link to web pages which are of reliable quality. Search engines, like the Web, are ever changing. What holds true today for a search engine may not do so in the future. A judgment at a point in time may not hold true for very long in the changing environment that is the World Wide Web. Search engines do not index all the documents on the Web, nor do they all index the same sites or in the same fashion.

WHY SUBJECT GATEWAYS IS IMPORTANT FOR TODAYS

Library web sites are becoming increasingly complex. Complexities in the form of links and services, profusion of print and electronic formats, duplication and the general web resources.

When the content becomes massive the functions of the library web sites needs more restructuring. This complex environment has arisen from various factors including: Innovative ways of providing information and services such as electronic resources, course specific, and library help pages and document delivery.

- Complex library searches due to the cross functions and links between the online catalogue, journal\aggregator databases, electronic resources etc..
- The need to identify and present high quality free information resources on the web and distinguish those from library licensed material.
- The increasing expectations of users for interfaces to lead directly, without undue hunting, to the information or service they need.
- Many library web sites get congested with ample content, general objectives and duplication of services. It is no longer simple and clears how to do research or projects with a tool that provides gateways for getting information. There are number of steps that a library researcher must perform to successfully get information. Thus Gateways are needed to improve the effectiveness of Internet searching and will serve as a source of information in specific areas and saves the time of the users.

CONCLUSION

Subject gateways are undoubtedly very useful Internet search tools. While they are more limited in the extent of their coverage than search engines, they are valued by users for the higher quality and relevance of their results. They have been particularly cited as a helpful starting point for Internet beginners to explore the resources available in a particular subject. All above gateways are specially relevant to library science those are in the field of multidisciplinary subject these are also related to library & information science which are useful for library professionals, users. The subject gateways have established a new trend in collaboration, which can only revitalise library service provision in the future.

REFERENCES

Campbell Debbie, Australian subject gateways - metadata as an agent of Change *http://www.nla.gov.au/nla/staffpaper/dca* mpbell2.html#feat

Dempsey, L. (2000). The subject gateway: experiences and issues based on the emergence of the Resource Discovery Network. *Online Information Review*, 24(1), 8-23.

Fischer, T., & Neuroth, H. (2000). SSG-FI - special subject gateways to high quality Internet resources for scientific users. *Online Information Review*, 24(1), 64-68.

Krishnamurthy, M "Digital library gateway for library and information science and study". *SRELS*

Koch, T. (2000). Quality-controlled subject gateways: definitions, typologies, empirical overview. *Online Information Review*, 24(1), 24-34.

Journal of Information Management. 39,3 (2002) Pp.245-254 Richard, B "Developing a web library: Guide for an academic library problems, solutions and future possibilities. " *Program* .31,1 1997), pp59-73

Tools for Information Retrieval on theInternethttp://eprints.rclis.org/archive/ Finding Information on the Internet: ATutorial, UC Berkeley - TeachingLibrary Internet Workshopshttp://www.lib.berkeley.edu/ TeachingLib/Guides/Internet/SearchEngines.html

Zeng M. L., & Chan, L. M. (2003). Trends and issues in establishing interoperability among knowledge organization systems. *Journal of the American Society for Information Science and Technology*, 55(5), 377-395.

17

Application of Total Quality Management in Library and Information Sectors

Ms. Sharmila Kumari
Ph.D Scholar , Deptt. of Lib&Information Science
Baba Mast Nath University, Rohtak

INTRODUCTION

Library and Information centers exist to support the learning and research needs of the institutions. These are dominant agencies for the dissemination of information. Their aim is to provide services acceptable to the users to their satisfaction. For successful functioning, these require professionals who arc not only to be professionally qualified, competent and efficient but also to be lively active, contended and well satisfied with their jobs. For sustaining the library services and librarianship, there is need to provide the library professional with adequate training in view of the rapid developments in the fields of science and technology.

In this changing scenario, library and information services

have to adapt to the new technique. In the process of adaptation, in all services and facilities units, a good quality assurance system plays an essential and important role in gearing up the library to provide users satisfaction. But failure to provide information professionals with adequate training and to deploy them effectively represents one of the constraints on change and development in library and information provisions and can undermine its effectiveness. This chapter will highlight the concept, management, benefits, barriers and suggestions of Total Quality Management in libraries and information sectors.

TOTAL QUALITY MANAGEMENT (TQM)

In the 1950s, the Japanese asked W.Edwards Deming, an American Statistician and management theorist, to help them improve their torn economy. By implementing Deming's principles of TQM, Japan experienced dramatic economic growth. In the 1980s, when the US began to see a reduction in its own world market share in relation to Japan, American business rediscovered Deming. Quality management experts, Joseph Juran and Philip Crosby, also contributed to the development of TQM theories, models and tools. TQM is now practiced in business as well as in government. the military, education, and in-profit organization including libraries

The concept of quality management originated in Japan and later moved into the USA and the UK, initially in the manufacturing sector. Since then, the theory of quality management has been growing fast. It has become a management philosophy in its own right and has taken shape in a series of international standards in the ISO 9000 series. The philosophy is increasingly being applied in the service sector, including libraries. Library and information managers (LIMB) arc these days deluged with advice as to how to acquire and organize teaming resources and satisfy the complex and ever-increasing information needs of their users. However, to achieve their goal, the question of a resource-constrained regime has to be kept in mind without sacrificing the interests of users. The services offered, accordingly, have to be internally efficient and externally effective. It is in this context that the question of "total quality" becomes relevant in the management of library and information services.

TOM CONCEPT

TQM is the art of managing the whole to achieve excellence. The golden rule is a simple but effective way to explain it. TQM is defined as a philosophy and a set of guiding principles that represent the foundations or a continuously improving organization. It is the application of qualitative methods and human resources to improve all the processes with an organisation and exceed customer needs now and in the future. TOM integrates fundamental management techniques, existing improvements, and technical tools under a disciplined approach.

Principles of Total Quality Management to enhance the library service. They are following:

1. Create service brochures and information kit;
2. Conduct a user survey about library service;
3. Improve signage;
4. Change hours of operation; Provide a more convenient material return;
5. Simplify check out of materials;
6. Use flexibility in staff assignments;
7. Cooperation with local governments;
8. Ask vendors to give product demonstrations;
9. Give new staff a thorough orientation;
10. Create interde' partmental library advisory groups;
11. Improve the physical layout of the library;
12. Track complaints;
13. Develop an active outreach programme;
14. Open satellite offices;

15. Publicize new or changed services;
16. Develop user and staff training materials;
17. Target services to specific groups;
18. Offer electronic document delivery;
19. Follow the mission statement; and
20. Smile.

BENEFITS OF TQM FOR LIBRARIES

1. TQM reduces bureaucracy, empower staff and create a team base culture, which is keenly desired and suited for mechanistic, hierarchical organizational structures like university libraries.
2. TQM helps in gauging users, needs and expectations in a proactive way and equips the librarian to provide more and better services with the same resources efficiently and effectively, resulting increased user satisfaction and loyalty.
3. TQM is an evolutionary process and can easily be incorporated into the already existing management system of libraries.
4. Brain storming exercises helps to know what functions are necessary to the efficient operation of a library and who should perform these, resulting increased employee involvement and dedication.
5. Reduction in. user complaint and gain a competitive advantage over other information providers.
6. TQM helps in breaking down intersectional barriers/status in a library and promotes cooperation and team work instead of competition.
7. In TQM quality is a high profile management tool. Its implementation in libraries improves the image of the library staff and helps in public relations and marketing.
8. TQM ensures consistent qualitative library & information services to users and defines user satisfaction issues.

9. TQM ensures a non-threatening environment for open debate for problem solving, for change, and clearly indicates power, responsibility and accountability of each employee.
10. Empowered staff members develop a sense of self determination: a sense Of meaning; sense of competence; a sense of impact and become more effective, innovative, transformational and charismatic.

BARRIERS FOR TQM IMPLEMENTATION

Four barriers which prevent the adoption of TQM in libraries. They are

(i) Vocabulary : Librarians are uncomfortable with the use of terms and concepts such as 'total', 'quality" management' which are affiliated with business & market place.

(ii) Resources : TQM demands long term commitment and the librarians are of the opinion that they cannot 'afford' to invest in the organization and implementation of quality programme.

(iii) Process : Our culture tends to be impatient and we try to solve problems quickly, contrary to TQM's careful process analysis.

(iv) Professionalism : Professional staff can be resistant to turning over their practices and services to what they perceive as the "uninformed whims of the customer".

Suggestions for Improving TQM in Libraries are following:

1. End the practice of awarding business on price tag alone. The lowest priced goods are not always the highest quality; choose a supplier based on its record of improvement and then make a long-term commitment to it.
2. Improve constantly and forever the system of product and service. Improvement is not a one-time effort; management is responsible for leading the organization into the practice of continual improvement in quality and productivity.

3. Institute training and retraining. Workers need to know how to do their jobs correctly even if they need to learn new skills.
4. Institute leadership. Leadership is the job of management. Managers have the responsibility to discover the barriers that prevent staff from, taking pride in what they do. The staff will know what these barriers are.
5. Drive out fear. People often fear reprisal if they "make waves" at work. Managers need to create an environment where workers can express concerns with confidence.
6. Break down barriers between staff areas. Managers should promote teamwork by helping staff in different areas/ departments work together. Fostering interrelationships among departments encourages higher quality decision-making.
7. Eliminate slogans, exhortations, and targets for the workforce. Using slogans alone, without an investigation into the processes of the workplace, can be offensive to workers because they imply that a better job could be done. Managers need to learn real ways of motivating people in their organizations.
8. Eliminate numerical quotas. Quotas impede quality more than any other working condition; they leave no room for improvement. Workers need the flexibility to give customers the level of service they need.
9. Remove barriers to pride of workmanship. Give workers respect and feedback about how they are doing their jobs.
10. Institute a vigorous program of education and retraining. With continuous improvement, job descriptions will change. As a result, employees need to be educated and retrained so they will be successful at new job responsibilities.
11. Take action to accomplish the transformation. Management must work as a team to carry out the previous 13 steps.

CONCLUSION

This paper has discussed the implementation of total quality management and its appl'cation to libraries. TQM demands time and persistence. To succeed in an organization there must be support at the very top and commitment at all leveis. It is necessary that all groups of people in an organization are included in the process. TQM implementation requires patience and tolerance as it is a time-consuming process and, of course, it is not easy to change an organization. Therefore, implementation of TQM is not a guarantee of the highest quality but it is a step in the right ditection. TQM implements a philosophy of strong leadership participation, increased communication among departments, and the education of all employees. TQM is proven to be profitable when implemented in a successful way, but there are also problems with the implementation. In the other word, there is a need for an increased focus on the area of organizational change related to TQM.

REFERENCES

1. Understanding Total Quality Management in Contest: Qualitative Research on Managers; Awareness of TQM Aspects in the Greek Service Industry by Alexandros G. Psychologios, The Qualitative Report Volume 12 Number 1 March 2007, pg 40-66.
2. P. R. Wadje, Total Quality Management, Journal of Textile Association, Jan.- Feb.,2006,pp 207-213.
3. Total Quality Management by, Devanand Uttam, National Conference on Advancements and Futuristic Trends in Mechanical and Material Engineering on 13th-14th,2006 at Department of Mechanical Engineering of G.Z.S. College of Engineering & Technology, Bathinda pg.4l 7-421.
4. Butcher, K.S. (1993). Total quality management: The Oregon State University Library's experience. "Journal of Library Administration," 18 (1/2), 45-56. (EJ 469 102)
5. Clack, M.E. (1993). Organisational development and TQM: The Harvard College Library's exprience. "Journal or Library Administration," 18 (1/2), 29-43. (EJ 469 101).
6. Deming, W.E. (1986), "Out of the Crisis." Cambridge, M.A. " Masschusetts institute of Technology, Center for Advanced Engineering Study.

7. DiMattia, E.A. Jr. (1993). Total Quality Management and Servicing Users through remote access technology. "Electronic Library, 11 (3), 187-191. (EJ 465 770)

8. Jurow, S & Barnard, S.B. (1993). Introduced: TQM fundamentals and overview of contents. " Journal of Library Administration, 18 (1/2), 1-13. EJ 469 099)

9. Mackey, T. & Mackey, K. (1992). Think quality The Deming approach does work in libraries. "Libraries Journal," 117 (9), 57-61. (EJ 446 234).

18

Digital Weds Virtual Library: A Critical View

Dr. Ashwani Kumar
Post-Doctoral Fellow, Dept. of Library and Information Science
Babasaheb Bhimrao Ambedkar University, Lucknow-226025

ABSTRACT

In information communication technology oriented era, most of the libraries has been computerized or going to be computerized, and moreover they have available for users their basic-services through the web or without web. Technological and economical changes in society made variations in the life style of people and this change drastically spreading in their mind & views because of this, their attitude are getting new innovative environment by which it goes towards electronic awareness which is moving from traditional to e-based or web based libraries. The access of any electronic library is totally based on the e-learning skill. The facility of the e-learning environment can be increase the literacy rate of the special as well as common people, because the e-learning environment and advent of ICT paved the way of digital library as well as virtual Library.

INTRODUCTION

Today we are surviving in ICT enable scenario where the society is gradually being digital. In ICT oriented environment,

Information technology is playing a significant role in the development of modern society. The escalating utilization of ICT has brought radical transforms in the library and information science field that has revolutionized change in whole scope of library and information services. Due to this the computerization of the library during past few decades have focused heavily on the creation of surrogate records of printed documents available in a library or for providing computerized services through secondary databases held locally on CD ROM or magnetic tapes. Digitization is occurring over every aspect of society and libraries are not exception to this phenomenon. The use of computers and computerization, information technology and digitization has been accepted by libraries and information centers.

The developing of digital libraries are attributed to digital resources, databases and capable to handle large amount of data and services to its users effectively in digital environment. While the terms digital libraries and electronic libraries are used interchangeably and synonymously, the term "virtual library" or "library without wall" usually refers to the Meta resources or subject portals that extend virtual accessibility of digital collections from several diverse sources without the users even knowing where the resource actually resides.

CONCEPTUAL DEFINITION OF DIGITAL AND VIRTUAL LIBRARY

- A digital library is popularly viewed as an electronic version of a library where storage is in digital form, allowing direct communication to obtain material and copying it from a master version. Rathore (2007)
- Digital Library contains all information in digital form means binary digits and includes CD & DVDs.

- The digital library is that place where information is selected, acquired, organized, stored and retrieved in digital form. So, digital library is an information services that provides all information resources in digital form.
- The Virtual Library is another kind of Digital Library which provides electronic platform to explore the information that is available electronically elsewhere. Anyone can access it from anywhere using internet.
- Virtual library is an organized set of links to items on the network..." (Charles Stuart University, n.d.)-

- Virtual Library contains electronic stocks including collection of full text of e-books, Journals and databases without any physical space or location. It is totally depended upon the Internet. Without Internet it cannot be accessed.

- "The concept of remote access to the contents and services of libraries and other information resources, combining an on-site collection of current and heavily used materials in both print and electronic form, with an electronic network which provides access to, and delivery from, external worldwide library and commercial information and knowledge sources". Gapen (1993)

CONCEPTUAL DIFFERENCE BETWEEN DIGITAL AND VIRTUAL LIBRARY

Virtual Library is "...an organized set of links to items on the network..." (Charles Stuart University, n.d.)-

Digital Library is "an information service in which all the information resources are available in computer process able form and the functions of acquisition, storage, retrieval, access and display are carried out through the use of digital technologies. Oppenheim and Smithson (1999:97)

DISTINGUISHED FEATURES OF A DIGITAL AND VIRTUAL LIBRARY

The features of the Digital and Virtual library are almost same but still have some technical differences which have given below:

1. A Digital Library is available wherever there is a personal computer connected to the network while The Virtual Library exist in cyberspace only, they have no buildings or shelves, all information materials are in digital format and are accessible via the Internet.
2. Digital Library provides access to very large information available or unavailable in physical collection while virtual library provide immediate access to a range of resources not available in physical collections.
3. Digital libraries are accessed by users through a single user-

friendly interface while a Virtual library provides speedy and wide access to updated information in a global manner.

4. Digital Library support multimedia content based on the electronic collection and Virtual Library Greater emphasis is on access and not on collection.
5. Digital Library and Virtual Library both are Time saving body.

COMPONENTS OF DIGITAL AND VIRTUAL LIBRARY

- Collection Infrastructure
- Digital Resource Organization
- Access Infrastructure
- Computer and Network Infrastructure
- IPR and Digital Rights Management
- Digital Library Services

PROCESS OF DIGITAL AND VIRTUAL LIBRARY

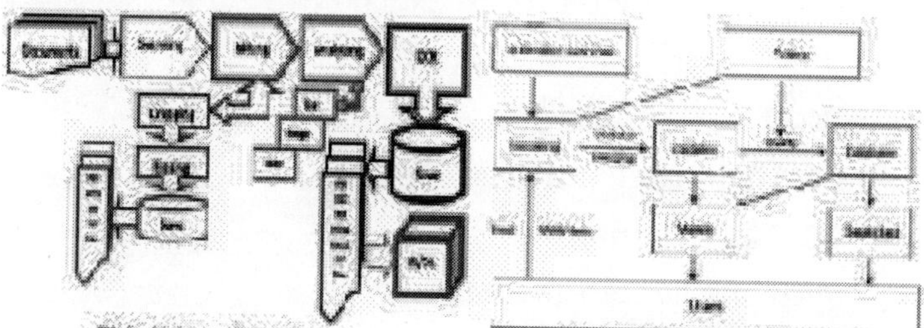

Digital Library Process

Virtual library Process

SERVICES OF DIGITAL LIBRARY AS WELL AS VIRTUAL LIBRARY

In electronic environment there are some common services of digital as well as virtual library include:

- OPAC to web PAC
- Digital Reference Service
- Library Chat Rooms
- Electronic Delivery Services

- Ask-A-Librarian
- Real Time Services
- Bulletin Boards
- SDI in Digital Library: Delivering Customized Contents
- RSS Feeds

Except it the virtual library creates virtual bibliographic and documentary services for users. Virtual library provided bibliographic searches, comprehensive documentary searches involving any subject of interest to the user.

DIGITAL AND VIRTUAL LIBRARIES: INDIAN SCENARIO

Library Consortium in India

- NDEST-AICTE Consortium (Govt.-funded)
- CSIR E-Journals Consortium (Govt-funded)
- UGC Info net Consortium (Govt.-funded)
- N-LJST
- DAE Consortium (Govt.-funded)
- MCIT Consortium (Govt.-funded)
- IIM Libraries Consortium
- FORSA Consortium
- Scholarly Science Journals
- Theses & Dissertations
- Vidyanidhi
- Shodhgang

In the context of virtual library the National Mission on Libraries (NML) (National Mission on Libraries i.e. High Level Committee set up by Ministry of Culture, Govt. of India) has given recommendation to up gradation of libraries providing service to the public". The scheme consists of some projects. The creation of Virtual Library is one of them.

The main purpose of **National Virtual Library of India** is to facilitate a comprehensive database and digital resources on information about India and on information generated in India, in an open access environment.

CONCLUSION

Today, in the perception of electronic environment it can be concluded that there are mainly three types of libraries exists viz. Electronic, Digital and Virtual Libraries (Difference between Electronic, Digital and Virtual Libraries, 2011). Digital libraries have been proved its relevancy to effective seeking of information and it is becoming more beneficial day by day to all academicians as well as academic bodies i.e. researchers, scholarly institutions and the entire research community. In the other hand it can be said that today most of the libraries, offer a wide range of on-line services to their users. In current ICT enable scenario, every academician is well acquainted with the internet and web technologies. So it is the suitable times for a Library to be digital as well as virtual and develop its on-line presence in order to instant fill up the gap feel by academicians. In this direction Virtual Libraries are the new visualization of the Libraries to make advance to ICT scenario in forthcoming days. it is assumed that Virtual Libraries may be provide a new way of serving the new generation users of the libraries. Virtual libraries are the new vision of libraries of the future. This paper provides critical view of a digital and virtual Library. It narrates conceptual definitions, differences, distinguish features, component, process and services and status of digital and virtual library.

REFERENCES

1. file:///C:/Users/ASHWANI/Downloads/42318-48670-1-SM.pdf accessed at 19 April 2018.
2. Gapen, K. G. (1993). The virtual library: Knowledge, society, and the librarian. In: L.M. Saunders (Ed.), The Virtual Library: Visions and Realities, pp.1-14. Westport: Meckler.
3. http://epgp.inflibnet.ac.in/ahl.php?csrno=21
4. http://ir.inflibnet.ac.in:8080/ir/bitstream/1944/1430/1/535-542.pdf accessed at 16 April 2018

5. http://www.nmlindia.nic.in/ accessed at 20 April 2018.
6. https://www.slideshare.net/dheerajsnegi9/virtual-libraries-empowering-tools-in-digital-environment accessed at 19 April 2018.
7. https://www.slideshare.net/NirmalSingh33/nirmal-42381186 accessed at 18 April 2018.
8. Koganurmath, Muttaya (2001) "From VIRTUAL LIBRARY: AN OVERVIEW" (Accessed from: http://ir.inflibnet.ac.in:8080/ir/bitstream/1944/1430/1/535-542.pdf at 19 April 2018.
9. Virtual Library: An Overview (PDF Download Available). Available from: https://www.researchgate.net/publication/228985156_Virtual_Library_An_Overview [accessed Apr 19 2018].